Drowning on Dry Land

A play

Alan Ayckbourn

Samuel French — London
www.samuelfrench-london.co.uk

Please see page iv for further copyright information

DROWNING ON DRY LAND

First performed at the Stephen Joseph Theatre, Scarborough, on the 4th May 2004, with the following cast:

Charlie Conrad	Stephen Beckett
Linzi Ellison	Melanie Gutteridge
Jason Ratcliffe	Adrian McLoughlin
Hugo de Préscourt, QC	Stuart Fox
Gale Gilchrist	Billie-Claire Wright
Marsha Bates	Sarah Moyle
Simeon Diggs	Paul Kemp

Directed by Alan Ayckbourn
Designed by Roger Glossop
Lighting by Mick Hughes

COPYRIGHT INFORMATION

(See also page ii)

CHARACTERS

Charlie Conrad, a celebrity, mid-thirties
Linzi Ellison, his wife, thirty-three
Jason Ratcliffe, his manager, fifties
Hugo de Préscourt QC, a barrister, forties
Gale Gilchrist, a TV journalist, mid-twenties
Marsha Bates, a children's entertainer, thirties
Simeon Diggs, her lawyer, forties
Laura, a girl of about ten (non-speaking)
Katie, a girl of about eight (non-speaking)

SYNOPSIS OF SCENES

The action of the play takes place in and around a folly in
Linzi's and Charlie's garden

ACT I An afternoon in June

ACT II
SCENE 1 An afternoon in August
SCENE 2 An afternoon in January

Time — the present

It is folly to drown on dry land
English proverb

ACT I

Linzi's and Charlie's garden somewhere in rural southern England, an hour or so's drive from London. A fine afternoon in June

It is a big, well-tended garden with a terrace, a lawn and, round at one side, a paddock. However, we don't see much of this, for what we are looking at is "The Folly", a nineteenth-century, stone-built circular tower. At ground level it is open in a stone-pillared semi-circle, to form a south-facing open seating area. There are three or four good-quality garden chairs and a low table in the semi-circle. At the back are two archways, each leading directly on to a shallow stairway, one going up, the other leading down. By some architectural sleight of hand (fortunately not one we are going to be called upon to explain!) the two are actually the same staircase. People attempting to climb the staircase through one doorway will find, despite an optical and sensory impression to the contrary, that they have actually climbed nowhere. Similarly, those who choose to descend will find that they, too, have miraculously remained on the same level

When the CURTAIN *rises the garden is lit with bright summer sunshine*

In a moment Linzi and Marsha enter from the direction of the house

Linzi is thirty-three. Outwardly, she has the good looks, poise and physical image that many women would happily kill for; but these do not satisfy Linzi. In her current restless, unhappy inner state she is given to changing her image on an almost daily basis

Marsha, in her thirties, is by contrast far less overtly glamorous. There is a nervousness and lack of confidence about her that has been accentuated by the glamour of her surroundings. She is dressed in her casual work clothes

It is apparent that whilst Marsha is doing her very best to impress her present temporary employer, Linzi is showing only scant interest in Marsha

Linzi … no, your best bet is to bring it up this way …
Marsha Yes, I will … I'm so sorry, I ——
Linzi … as I say, you should have parked round the side of the house there …

Marsha Yes, I realize now I should have done that. I should have realized ...

Linzi We always keep that side by the kitchen clear for, you know, staff and that ...

Marsha Yes, it was silly of me ...

Linzi ... for tradespeople and suchlike ...

Marsha ... I should have thought ...

Linzi You could have parked next to the catering vans. We only allow parking down there in the paddock just for today ...

Marsha Yes, yes ...

Linzi ... overflow parking ...

Marsha ... for the party, yes, of course.

Linzi That's normally the paddock. We had to move the pony, of course.

Marsha Oh, how lovely! You've got a pony! Is that your son's pony?

Linzi No, it's Jade's. Harry's baby sister's. It's her pony ...

Marsha Ah! And how old is she?

Linzi Four and a half.

Marsha Heavens! Her own pony already! Lucky little girl!

Linzi Well, you know, kids. Once Harry got his little racing car ...

Marsha I always wanted a pony. Always.

Linzi (*abstracted*) And the trampoline ...

Marsha But my parents couldn't ... You call him Harry, do you? Your son? He's known as Harry?

Linzi He prefers Harry. We don't call him Horsham. Not normally.

Marsha No.

Linzi That's only for the newspapers and that.

Marsha Yes. Well, that's easier, I suppose. Harry. Easier than Horsham.

Linzi (*gazing into the distance*) Harry doesn't like Horsham ...

Marsha What made you call him Horsham?

Linzi Sorry?

Marsha Why Horsham?

Linzi (*vaguely*) No ...

Pause. Linzi seems miles away. Marsha gazes upwards.

Marsha Quite a tower this. Very high. Unusual. (*Pause*) Wonderful view. I should imagine. From the top. (*Pause*) What date was it built, do you know?

Linzi (*coming out of her reverie*) Listen, do you mind if I leave you to collect your stuff on your own ... ?

Marsha No, of course.

Linzi Only I need to get on. All these people arriving ...

Marsha Yes. How many children are you expecting?

Linzi (*vaguely*) Kids? About seventy, I think.

Marsha (*a bit taken aback*) Heavens.

Linzi If they all turn up. Then there's the parents on top of that, of course. Getting on for two hundred, all told. We usually try and limit it to two hundred.

Marsha Goodness! Some birthday party ... Lucky little boy.

Linzi Well, it's only once a year, isn't it? (*Pause*) Right.

Marsha (*realizing she is being dismissed*) Right. (*Turning to go*) I'll go and ...

Linzi You can cope with seventy, can you? You'll be all right with seventy?

Marsha Yes, it's a few more than I'm ... but fine ...

Linzi I mean, we could split them ...

Marsha I mean, usually there aren't quite so ...

Linzi We did for the fire-eater a couple of years ago ...

Marsha ... no, it'll be fine. I'll just do my broader stuff, don't worry ...

Linzi Angie said you could probably cope.

Marsha Yes, it was so kind of Mrs Spencer-Fullerton to recommend me, I ——

Linzi You need a hand then, will you? With your gear?

Marsha No, that's all right ...

Linzi I can call someone ...

Marsha No, no. I'm used to it.

Linzi Just as you like ...

Pause. Linzi still shows no sign of going

Marsha Right, I'll ... (*She makes to leave again, then stops. Rather tentatively*) — Er ...

Linzi Yes?

Marsha Excuse me for asking ... but will your husband be here today?

Linzi Charlie? He's around somewhere, I think ... I hope he is.

Marsha I'm just — I'm just, I'm such a fan of his ...

Linzi (*uninterested*) That's nice ...

Marsha I'd so love to meet him. He's my — I think I am genuinely his absolute number one fan. I think he's just — What I like about him, you see, is he's not like other celebrities, is he? ... You know, some of them, you know, you can't relate to ... not at all ... I mean, some of them are great but they're not like ordinary people. If you see what I mean. Whereas your husband, he always comes over as so — *normal*. Do I mean that? Perhaps I mean ordinary? No, I don't mean ordinary, I mean normal. I'd so much like to meet him. Just to tell people I've — Is he like that to live with? He must be.

Linzi Like what?

Marsha You know, normal?
Linzi Pardon?
Marsha (*confused*) I must get on. Excuse me.

Marsha goes off towards the garden

Linzi stands staring after Marsha, frowning

In a moment Jason, a man of around fifty, appears through one of the archways at the back of the tower. He is casually but expensively dressed

Linzi scarcely listens to the following

Jason (*seeing Linzi as he appears*) … you know, it's amazing, that is, Linzi. Every time I come here, it gets me every time. That is brilliant, that is. Whoever designed that was a genius, wasn't he? I mean, when you think about it, eighteen — When was this built, Linzi? Eighteen-eighty — whatever — I mean, when you think about it — in some respects, we've not moved on since those days, have we? Not really. I mean, yes, in some ways, yes. We've got cars, we've got planes, we've got computers, television, light bulbs, mobile phones, you know, all of that — whatever. But in other ways, we haven't really moved on, that's my point. Have we? Not when it comes to design like that. It's amazing. (*He stares back at the passageway*) I don't know how it works. Mathematical, it must be. Don't ask me. I still can't work it out. Sheer brilliance. (*He studies the archway some more*)

Silence

Linzi (*who has scarcely been listening to this*) I'm really pissed off, you know that, Jason?
Jason Mind you, the ancient Chinese did it all before anyway, didn't they?
Linzi You hear me?
Jason What's that?
Linzi I said, I'm really pissed off. I really am. Seriously, Jason.
Jason Well …
Linzi He knew this party was today. He knew it was. You both did. He knows when his own son's birthday is, for Christ's sake. Now he's not going to be there, is he? What am I going to tell Harry? The first thing he'll say is, "Where's Dad? Where's me dad?" He's bound to. What am I going to tell him?
Jason You'll be there, though, won't you?
Linzi I'll be there, yes. I'm always there. He doesn't want me, does he? He's a boy, he wants his dad. He doesn't want me. I could walk out tomorrow, Harry'd never notice.

Jason Ah, come on ——

Linzi 'Cos it's me who has to tell him off all the time, it's left to me, isn't it? Tell him not to do things. It should be his dad doing that, only it's left to me, isn't it? Charlie? He just sits there, smiling. "Oh come on, he's only a lad, Linzi, give him a chance. I was a lad once." He pushed his sister in the swimming pool the other day. She nearly drowned. "Oh, come on, he's only larking about, Linzi. He's just a lad, isn't he?" That's what lads do, apparently. Try and drown their baby sisters.

Jason Don't get in a state, Linzi. This was the only day we could arrange it, I've said. The only day Charlie was free. You know what it's like.

Linzi But he wasn't free, was he? That's the point. He should have been at his son's birthday party, that's what I'm saying. Six years old, his dad should be there. I blame you for this just as much. I blame you too, Jason.

Jason Look, if you don't believe me, I'll show you Charlie's diary. He hasn't got a spare minute between now and Christmas, Linzi.

Linzi Well, I'm telling you now, both of you, I'm not sticking it much longer, I'm really not —— (*She breaks off as she sees Marsha returning from the garden*))

Marsha enters carrying her prop hamper

Marsha (*a little breathlessly*) Excuse me. Yes. Excuse me. (*To Jason, shyly*) Afternoon.

Jason How d'you do.

Marsha exits to the house

Linzi and Jason watch her

Jason Who's that, then?

Linzi She's the — entertainer. You know. For the kids. Angie recommended her.

Jason Ah.

Linzi I hope she can handle them. She seems a bit quiet. Shy.

Jason Well, they often are. Entertainers. Shy. Off stage.

Linzi I never met any. I mean, kids at that age, they're animals. If she's shy with them, they'll have her for tea.

Jason She'll be fine.

Linzi I'll tell you this much, Jason. Just 'cos I've had his kids, I don't plan to spend the rest of my life being a mother, I'll tell you that. (*Irritably*) Where is he, then?

Jason Who?

Linzi Charlie. I thought you were doing an interview out here.

Jason No, it's just a meeting. Preliminary. Charlie wanted to meet out here. Interview's not for two weeks.

Linzi Well, where is he? I want a word with him.
Jason Woman hasn't arrived yet, has she?
Linzi So where is he?
Jason On the phone, I think.
Linzi Who to?
Jason I don't know.
Linzi Who're you meeting, anyway?
Jason Gale Gilchrist.
Linzi Gale Gilchrist?
Jason Didn't he tell you?
Linzi (*alarmed*) For God's sake, you're not bringing that woman down here?
Jason Didn't he tell you?
Linzi Charlie? He never tells me anything. He's never here, is he? Gale Gilchrist?
Jason She's all right …
Linzi … she's a monster.
Jason I can handle Gale, don't worry.
Linzi What about Charlie? Can he handle her?
Jason I'll be with him.
Linzi You better had be, Jason, that's all. Why the hell are you letting her come here? Into our home, for God's sake?
Jason Because it's Gale Gilchrist. She's a major player these days, you know that, Linzi. Her viewing figure's off the scale. With Charlie's new sponsorship deal in the pipeline, we could do with her right now.
Linzi She destroys people. That's how she's built her reputation.
Jason And they all love her. Currently she's walking on water …
Linzi You saw what she did to Ronnie the other week. I've heard the BBC aren't renewing his contract now …
Jason Well, that would have all come out sooner or later, anyway, wouldn't it? Ronnie's funny habits. It wasn't exactly the world's best secret, was it? Everybody knew. Didn't need Gale. Once the police confiscated his computer, Ronnie was fair game.
Linzi Well, I'm not talking to her. I tell you, I'm not even saying hallo to her ——
Jason (*soothingly*) Now, Linzi, you can't do that, you know that …
Linzi — and you keep her away from my kids, as well. Poisonous little bitch.
Jason Listen! Listen! Linzi! When she arrives, you and Charlie give her a nice warm welcome, all right?
Linzi No way …
Jason There's nothing she can say about Charlie, is there? Either of you. Unless you give her something. You two greet her — the world's perfect couple ——
Linzi Oh, yes?

Jason Yes! "Welcome to our beautiful home. Now, I must get back to my party, excuse me." That's all you have to say. That's all it is.
Linzi That's all she's getting. From me.
Jason As for Charlie, we don't need to worry about him. There's nothing there for her, is there? That's the joy with Charlie. Mr Clean. No worries, no scandals. He's like a pane of glass, that lad. Nothing to hide. You can see straight through him, can't you? Sheet of glass.
Linzi Yes, like a mirror. Most days you end up talking to your own reflection.

Jason looks at her for a moment

Jason You're in a funny mood today, aren't you?
Linzi I've told you. I've had enough of it.

Marsha appears, making another journey from the house

Marsha (*smiling at them*) Excuse me. One more trip ...
Linzi — er — listen, dear, when you do your act, like ... You're able to talk louder than that, are you?
Marsha Sorry?
Linzi Louder. When you're performing? Because there's quite a few kids and they can be quite noisy. Some of them. I mean, I think we could find you a microphone, if you'd like one. Save your voice.
Marsha (*a little alarmed*) Oh, no. He never speaks.
Linzi Pardon?
Marsha Chortles. Mr Chortles the Clown, he never speaks. He's a mime, you see ...
Linzi He's a what?
Marsha A mime. He's a clown. Mr Chortles expresses himself entirely through silent physicality. He has no need of speech. Didn't Mrs Spencer-Fullerton tell you?
Linzi No, she didn't.
Marsha (*anxiously*) That's not a problem, is it? I mean, you weren't expecting a stand-up, were you? I mean, jokes and things?
Linzi No, I'm sure you'll be fine. It was just the magician we had last year, he was very loud indeed. They could hear him in Dorset.
Marsha Well, I do find as a general rule that the louder you are as a performer, the noisier the children tend to become ...
Linzi (*doubtfully*) Oh, yes?
Marsha But that's just my personal experience ... Sorry. Excuse me.

Marsha exits again to the garden

Linzi and Jason watch her go

Linzi I'd better alert security, she's going to need rescuing, I can feel it.

Jason You won't let me down now, will you, Linzi? When Gale Gilchrist arrives? You'll do your bit, won't you? Know what I mean?

Linzi I won't let you down, Jason, don't worry. I know my place after seven years. Little wife, little mother. All loving smiles. Don't worry.

Jason (*anxiously*) Things are all right, aren't they? Between you and Charlie?

Linzi Ecstatic.

Jason No problems? You know …?

Linzi What, sexual, you mean?

Jason Well, I don't know …

Linzi You can't possibly have sexual problems, Jason, with someone you only see once every other month …

Jason It's not that bad.

Linzi It is that bad. I'm telling you.

Jason What can I say? Charlie's on a roll, Linzi. You want him to stop in his tracks? Drop everything? Listen, he's not a novelist or a painter or a musician, is he? He's a personality. And when he does finally stop, he won't leave anything behind except a few feet of videotape. He won't have a back catalogue, not like the Beatles. He has to cash it all in now, Linzi, you know that. He steps off now, he'll never get back on. No way.

Linzi You needn't tell me, Jason. I know that. I know all about stepping off.

Jason (*guiltily*) Well, yes, I'm — as I said, Linzi, I am making enquiries. See if I can find an opening for you to, like, get you back in … But it has to be right, doesn't it? You've got a high profile now, Linzi. I mean you're Mrs Charlie Conrad now, you can't do just anything, can you?

Linzi (*angrily*) I'm not Mrs Charlie Conrad, I'm Linzi Ellison!

Jason All right, sorry …

Linzi I've never been Mrs Conrad. You know that, Jason! Never. Not even in the local village, I'm not. I hate that.

Jason Yes, well, whatever. That's how several million people think of you. And frankly, it's — it's been seven years, Linzi … and seven years in this business — it's a question of reminding people. Reintroducing you. There's a whole new set of people since your day. Programme controllers, producers — they change overnight, you know that. And most of them are about fourteen years old. It's frightening. But we'll find something. Don't worry, we'll find something. Takes time, that's all.

Linzi Well, I'm thirty-three and I'm running out of that, Jason. I miss it. I don't mind admitting. I never thought I would, but I do. But I never would have — if I'd known … I used to be like Charlie, didn't I? Well, almost. Every time I went out of the front door there were people coming up to me, smiling, recognizing me, special treatment in the supermarket, all that. And I didn't think I'd miss it. I really didn't. I was happy to pack it all in, marry Charlie, have kids, be a wife and a mother. But six and a half years and — I'm nobody, Jason. I'm just an extension of Charlie, that's all I am. Charlie Conrad's wife, you're right.

Jason You know I didn't mean that ——

Linzi No, you're right. I used to be somebody. These days, I go out, no-one even notices me half the time. I used to matter, Jason, in my own right. That's all I'm saying. These days I don't matter. I don't even matter to the kids half the time and I certainly don't matter to Charlie.

Jason (*slightly alarmed*) You don't suspect he's … ?

Linzi How do you mean, with someone else? No. He gets plenty of offers, I'm sure he does. But no. (*She reflects*) Almost be better if he was.

Jason With another woman?

Linzi Stir things up a bit, anyway.

Jason God forbid. Bring the whole lot down, that would.

Linzi (*smiling*) Maybe he'll go off with Gale Gilchrist.

Jason (*smiling*) Somehow, I think not. A little unlikely.

Linzi She's that ruthless. She'd do anything for an interview, I hear.

Jason Not Charlie. I've known him too long for that.

Linzi Not as long as I have.

Jason True.

Linzi If it hadn't been for me, you'd never have even got him, would you?

Jason Probably not.

Linzi Not probably. You wouldn't. No, I think you owe me, Jason.

Jason You're still my client, Linzi. I've still got your picture on my office wall, I promise.

Linzi About time you turned it round the right way, then.

Charlie enters from the direction of the house. He is in his mid-thirties, tall, good-looking and easy-natured. Again, he is casually dressed but every-thing about him says money. He carries a mobile

Charlie (*cheerfully*) Hi.

Linzi Where've you been, then?

Charlie Talking to Jack. He's doing some commercial in Spain.

Linzi How is he?

Charlie No idea. I think he was drunk. I couldn't make out what he was talking about, actually … Where's this woman, then?

Jason On her way.

Charlie I thought we were meeting at two?

Jason She's stuck in traffic. She's going to give me another call when she gets to the village.

Linzi In that case you can look in at the party, can't you?

Charlie I said, I can't ——

Linzi Just for half an hour. Say hallo to the guests. Reintroduce yourself to
  your children. Wish your son a happy birthday. Wouldn't that be nice?
Charlie I did that. I did that this morning.
Linzi You weren't here this morning.
Charlie First thing. I woke him up.
Linzi You were in London this morning.
Charlie On his mobile, I called Harry on his mobile.
Linzi That's not the same, is it?
Charlie Sang him "Happy Birthday".
Linzi That's not the same. Six years old. He shouldn't even have a mobile
  at his age.
Charlie He wanted one.
Linzi He wanted his face tattooed and a tongue-pierce but he didn't get one,
  did he?
Charlie That's different.
Linzi I told him he had to wait till he was ten. Once he's ten he can punch
  holes wherever he likes, what do I care?
Charlie You changed your hair again.
Linzi Since when?
Charlie Since I last saw you. Since Thursday.
Linzi I've had it touched up, yes.
Charlie It's a completely different colour.
Linzi (*a little sharply*) At least you noticed, darling, that makes a change.

Silence. Charlie stares at Linzi

Jason Suits you. That colour.

A moment. Jason's mobile rings

  This could be her. (*Checking the phone*) Yes, it is. (*Answering*) Hallo. ...
  Gale? ... Where are you, darling? ... Oh, dear ... All right. Just a second,
  I'll direct you ... (*He heads to the house. Covering the phone for a second*)
  You two. Sweetness and light, right? (*Uncovering the phone again*) Gale,
  darling. ... sorry about that. ... now. ... if you're in the High Street which
  way are you pointing, my love? ... Yes. ... Yes. ...

  Jason goes off

A silence. After a moment, Charlie moves to Linzi

Charlie Linzi ... (*He touches her arm gently*)
Linzi Don't.

Charlie Don't what?
Linzi Don't.
Charlie (*withdrawing his hand*) Oh, Jesus!

Charlie moves away from her unhappily. He wanders to one of the archways at the back of the Tower and disappears through it

Marsha returns with a large suitcase

Marsha (*to Linzi*) Last lot … (*Indicating her suitcase*) Costume. (*She laughs*)

Linzi doesn't react. She is abstracted again, barely noticing Marsha

Right. I'd better get a move on. Get changed. Do my stretches. I always need a minute or two, just to allow Mr Chortles to take over. (*She laughs again*)

Linzi does not respond

I know, it must sound weird, I know it must do, but when I'm working I become inhabited by Mr Chortles. Possessed, if you like. Invaded. He completely takes me over, you see. This — anarchic someone — who's no longer me. Do you follow? I can do all sorts of things when he's in me, as it were — when Mr Chortles is me — that I, me, Marsha Bates, could never do in a million years. Never dare to do. But Marsha becomes a totally other person. She *is* Mr Chortles. Spiritually as well as physically.

Charlie emerges from the same archway he left by

Actually, I sort of half-believe that in a previous life I was very probably … Oh.

Marsha notices Charlie for the first time. She stares, tongue-tied

Charlie (*smiling at her*) Hi.
Marsha I — er — oh — I — I — mmmm …

Silence

Mmmm. Mmm. I'm so — can't … Incredible … believe it … mmmm … mmm … mmm …

Silence

Linzi (*bored*) This is my husband, Charlie. Charlie, this is Maisie ——
Marsha Marsha ——
Linzi — who's going to entertain the children this afternoon. Including your son and your daughter.
Charlie (*smiling*) Oh. Right. (*To Marsha*) Thanks for coming. Hope it all goes well for you.
Marsha I'm ... I'm — um — er ... I can't just ... to me ...
Charlie Been doing this for long, have you? Entertaining kids?
Marsha ... mmmm ...
Charlie Tell you what, if you want to pop back later, bring something you'd like me to sign, I'll give you an autograph, OK? If you'd like.
Marsha ... mmmmmmm ... (*She stands gazing at Charlie like an eager, quivering puppy*)
Linzi (*rather impatiently*) Time's getting on, dear. I think you should start getting ready, don't you, dear?
Marsha ... mmmm ... (*She backs away from Charlie, loath to take her eyes off him, during the following*)

Charlie continues to smile at Marsha

Linzi Listen, if you come back down this way, round about quarter to, we'll get them all sitting in rows on the back lawn. Then you can enter from behind the hedge, there. Along the terrace. All right? Can you hear me?
Marsha (*who is still retreating*) ... mmm ...
Charlie (*still smiling at Marsha*) Cheers, then! See you later.
Marsha ... mmm ...

Marsha goes off to the house at last

Silence

Linzi (*as she goes*) Oh, for God's sake!
Charlie She be all right with the kids, you think? Seems a bit shy.
Linzi You're not coming down to Harry's party, I take it?
Charlie I've got this meeting, haven't I?
Linzi You promised you'd judge the fancy dress.
Charlie Fancy dress!
Linzi For Jade. Jade loves dressing up, you know that. Look, all those people, Charlie, they've only come to meet you, you know, most of them.

Pause

Well, you can at least give the prize. Take you five minutes.

Charlie If we finish in time. I'll try.

Linzi Which means no, doesn't it? Well, fuck you, Charlie. That's all I can say. Fuck you! (*She heads for the garden*)

Jason enters with Gale, who is still in her twenties, attractive and charming; the most dangerous sort of media personality. At present she is on a major high. She is carrying a handbag

Jason Here she is!

Gale So sorry, everyone, I'm sorry, sorry, sorry.

Linzi's and Charlie's manner and body language alter quite suddenly. Linzi returns to Charlie and they link arms, instantly the smiling, happy couple

Gale (*taking in this picture*) Oh! And there they both are, just look at them, bless them. Hallo, you gorgeous pair. Hi! Hi! Hi!

Charlie (*smiling*) Hi!

Linzi (*smiling*) Hallo!

Gale What about all this, then? You lucky people! Isn't it just beautiful? It's stunning. And look, you've even got your own Tower, my God, you've got your own Tower as well. It's fantastic! Hallo, Charlie Conrad, I cannot tell you how thrilled I am to meet you, I really am. Gale Gilchrist! Hi!

Charlie Hi.

Linzi Hallo.

Gale When I told the girls in the office I was going to be meeting Charlie Conrad this weekend, they were green. I tell you they were green. Hallo, you must be Lindy. Gale Gilchrist! Hi!

Linzi Linzi.

Gale Hi! Tell me, how does it feel, Lindy, to be hated by every woman in the country?

Linzi Linzi. It's Linzi.

Gale Linzi. Linzi, God, sorry. Of course, it's Linzi. Linzi, Linzi, Linzi! How does it feel, tell me?

Linzi Well, you get used to it after a bit, you ——

Gale I had this nightmare journey. Is the traffic always that bad? On that motorway bit?

Charlie At weekends it can be.

Gale Are you both totally happy here? You must be. You must never want to leave here, surely?

Linzi Yes, in summer especially, yes, it's ——

Gale I'd never want to leave. If I lived here, I'd never, never leave, I know I wouldn't. So what was this place originally? It's so unusual.

Jason This is a genuine Victorian folly, Gale.

Gale Wow! Would you believe?

Charlie We use it as a summer-house mostly. It's a listed building, so we can't do much with it.

Jason Eighteen eighty-something or other, isn't it?

Charlie Eighty-something.

Linzi Eighteen eighty-seven.

Gale Whatever! Who's counting?

Jason It's particularly unusual, though, Gale. Built by this industrialist, wasn't it, Charlie? From up north somewhere.

Charlie Middlesbrough.

Linzi Huddersfield.

Charlie Huddersfield.

Gale Huddersfield! Fantastic!

Jason Only when his wife died, this industrialist sold up. He sold his mill, retired, remarried and came south. What was his name? Terence — something, wasn't it?

Charlie Terence Harwood.

Linzi Hartford.

Charlie Terence Hartford.

Linzi Thomas Hartford.

Charlie Right.

Gale God, fantastic! And he built the house?

Jason No, the house was already here, wasn't it, Charlie? That's even earlier than this Tower, isn't it? The house is early eighteen-something ...

Charlie Eighteen thirty-something.

Gale Fantastic!

Charlie Edwardian.

Linzi Georgian.

Charlie Right.

Linzi Eighteen twenty-three.

Gale Whatever. Who's counting? It must have a brilliant view. This Tower?

Jason (*winking*) Well, it's an interesting one, wouldn't you say, Charlie?

Charlie (*smiling*) Quite interesting, yes.

Jason Would you like to climb up and have a look before we get started, Gale?

Gale (*looking at them, sensing there may be a trick to this*) Well ...

Charlie Go on, have a look.

Gale No, I'm sure you don't ——

Jason Linzi, why don't you give Gale a quick tour up the Tower before we start?

Charlie Good idea.

Gale Well ...

Linzi I'm sure Gale doesn't really want to ——

Jason Go on. We can wait.
Gale Well. If you're sure. If it's no trouble, I'd love to have a quick look.
Linzi Follow me, then.
Gale Just a quick one.

Linzi leads Gale to the "up" stairway

(*Examining both stairways, as she follows*) Oh, I see. You can go up or down, can you? Fantastic ...
Linzi After you.
Gale (*a little warily*) Nothing's going to jump out at me, is it?
Linzi Nothing like that. Promise. It's quite a gentle climb.
Gale (*going through the archway*) It's very dark.
Linzi Don't worry, there's plenty of light once your eyes get accustomed ...

Linzi follows Gale off along the passageway. Their voices are heard echoing and receding

Gale (*off; echoing*) Fantastic! How high do we climb exactly?
Linzi (*off; echoing*) I'm not sure. About a hundred feet, probably.
Gale (*off; echoing, making ghostly noises*) Woooo! Hooo! Hooo! Hooo!

Charlie laughs

Jason Don't be fooled by her, Charlie. She's a bright girl, that one.
Charlie I know that.
Jason Ambitious. Don't let your guard down. Remember, she needs us more than we need her. Her show's doing OK but she's vulnerable. You can't keep on pissing on people week after week.
Charlie (*shrugging*) I've got nothing to hide.
Jason I hope you haven't.
Charlie How do you mean?

The atmosphere becomes awkward and a little tense. These are not matters that the two normally discuss

Jason (*awkwardly*) Charlie, I know you don't like to talk about these things but you're both—you and Linzi ... Well. You're having a ... You're going through a bit of a ... Aren't you? Just at present?
Charlie No.
Jason Linzi says you are.
Charlie (*equally awkwardly*) Oh, you know Linzi. She has these ... But they ... Eventually.

Jason I think there may be more — more to it than that, Charlie, I really do.
I think maybe you ought to find time to — you know …
Charlie What?
Jason You know. Talk to her.
Charlie I do talk to her. I'm always talking to her. Most of the time she
doesn't listen. I tell her what I've been up to. Where I've been. I tell her who
I've met. All sorts of interesting things.
Jason Good. That's good.
Charlie Only she's not interested.
Jason Well, have you thought — maybe you're not talking to her about the
right things, Charlie?
Charlie How do you mean?
Jason Well. Like — talking to her about the things she needs to talk about.
Things like that.
Charlie Things like what?
Jason Well. Like — her, for instance. Maybe she needs to talk about her.
Occasionally.

Silence. Charlie considers this

(*Apologetically*) Anyway. What do I know?
Charlie We do talk about her. Occasionally. But with Linzi, it's — I don't
know — it's difficult, you know …
Jason Why's that?
Charlie Well, there's not that much to talk about, is there? She doesn't do
much these days. Except look after the kids. It's a bit boring.
Jason Maybe you should try taking her out?
Charlie I would. But she doesn't want to come. Not any more. There's
nothing to stop her. Look, we've got nannies, we've got *au pairs*, we've
got cleaners, we've got — housekeepers, gardeners, we've got everything.
There's literally nothing for her to do here. She could come. I've offered.
But she won't come.
Jason Why? Why do you think that is?
Charlie She says she doesn't feel easy. Going out with me. Not any more.
She says no one knows who she is. I say to her, you're my wife, for God's
sake. That's who you are. And I'm proud of you. And I want to show you
off a bit. To people. You know.
Jason Right.
Charlie But for some reason, she thinks she's boring. I keep telling her she's
not but — I don't think she believes me.
Jason Well.
Charlie You ever have that problem with Judy, do you?
Jason No. Not with Judy. She never goes out, anyway.

The sound of the women's voices is now heard approaching from the other stairwell

Gale (*off; echoing*) ... God, are we near the top yet?
Linzi (*off; echoing*) Keep going. Not much further ...
Jason (*as he and Charlie hear this*) Here they come.
Gale (*off; echoing*) Oh, look, yes. I can see light. I can see daylight up ahead, I think.
Linzi (*off; echoing*) Keep going, then.
Gale (*off; approaching*) The view must be fantastic, especially on a day like today. You should be able to see for mi — Oh!

Gale appears in the other archway, climbing the last few stairs and entering the Tower only a few feet away from where she started her journey

(*Seeing the men*) My God, how did you get up here before us — we ...? (*She breaks off. She stares around, momentarily disoriented*)

Linzi emerges behind her

(*Staring around her*) But we're — we haven't — we're in exactly the — that is extraordinary! That is *weird*! That is so *weird*! I could have sworn we were climbing. I was totally convinced we were climbing.
Jason Odd, isn't it? Odd feeling.
Gale But we were. We were climbing.
Linzi No, it's an illusion.
Charlie You're actually on the same level all the time.
Linzi But because of the steps you convince yourself you're climbing ...
Jason It's the clever way with the bricks as well. The way they're laid out.
Charlie Same as with the high windows.
Gale It's amazing. Quite amazing. It had me completely fooled.
Jason It does most people. First time, anyway. You're told you're climbing, everything tells you you're climbing, so you convince yourself you must be climbing.
Gale So there's actually no way up to the top at all?
Charlie No.
Jason They say there is but no one's ever ... Hallo, hallo there. Who's this, then?

Two young girls, Laura and Katie, aged about ten and eight years old respectively, enter from the direction of the garden, hand in hand. They are wearing party dresses

Linzi (*seeing them*) Hey! Hey! Hey! What are you two doing up here? You shouldn't be here, should you?

*Linzi moves to them and takes them by the hand. The girls stare at Charlie
in fascination*

Charlie Hallo, then!

Linzi This is Laura. And this is Katie, isn't it? They both live next door, don't
   you?

Gale Hallo, Katie! Hallo, Laura!

Jason Hallo, there.

Linzi (*to the girls*) Come on, we must go back or we'll miss the party, won't
   we? (*To the others*) Please excuse us … (*To the girls*) Come on, you two.
   (*To the others*) See you later.

Gale See you later.

Linzi (*sweetly, to Charlie*) Darling, you will remember you promised you'd
   give the fancy-dress prize, won't you?

Charlie Ah, yes …

Linzi I'm sure you can slip away for five minutes. Can't he?

Gale Of course. We can all come and watch, can't we?

Jason Yes.

Linzi If it's difficult I can always bring the winners up here.

Charlie No, no, I'll ——

Linzi (*blowing a kiss*) See you later then, darling.

Charlie (*likewise*) See you later, darling.

Jason (*murmuring to Gale*) Inseparable. They're inseparable …

Gale (*not altogether convinced by this*) Yes … Divine little girls!

Linzi exits in the direction of the garden with Laura and Katie

Gale What's going on? A birthday party, did you say?

Charlie Yes. For Harry. He's six today.

Gale This is your son, Horsham?

Charlie Right.

Gale What on earth made you choose to call him Horsham?

Charlie Well, it was either that or Wisborough Green.

Gale I see.

Charlie We weren't really looking out of the car window at the time. (*He
   winks at her*)

Gale (*smiling*) No.

Charlie We were being driven, mind you.

Gale (*smiling*) Glad to hear it.

Jason (*anxious to break this up*) Yes, well, time's getting on. Do you think
   we should … ?

Gale (*her attention back on the Tower*) Who on earth would build something
   like this? It must have cost a fortune even in those days.

Jason Well, apparently the Thomas Hartford bloke, when he moved down here with his new young wife, she suffered from a fear of heights, you see. Vertigo, you know. So he built her this tower. Lucy's Tower. Which she could climb and never get dizzy.

Gale (*dubious*) Is that true, do you think?

Jason Probably not.

Charlie It could be. He was madly in love apparently.

Gale Or just mad. And there's no way up to the top, you say?

Charlie There's meant to be. We've never found one. I've crawled all over it.

Jason If there is, you'd need to knock it down to find it.

Charlie Only it's listed.

Jason And if you did that and there wasn't one, you'd look pretty stupid and all.

Gale Weird.

A slight pause

Gale Still. I know you've got a lot to do, Charlie, so I won't keep you too long.

Jason You want to sit down, Gale?

Gale (*sitting and rummaging in her bag*) Thank you. This is just a preliminary chat really, just to establish the areas we want to talk about; and equally the areas you'd prefer not to talk about. Et cetera, et cetera, you know. You've done this a hundred rimes before, Charlie, I don't need to tell you, do I?

Charlie and Jason sit

(*Producing a small recording device*) I hope you don't object to my using this thing. The point is, with these interviews, I'm unusual, I seldom use a researcher. Well, only for the very basics. But the main slog I prefer to do myself. So this is just a reminder, for me, when I get back. You don't mind, do you?

Jason Not in the least. (*Producing a similar device from his pocket*) You won't object to this one either, will you? Just to make doubly sure.

Gale (*playfully*) Oh, Jason! Suspicious boy, you. (*Switching on her machine briefly*) Testing! Charlie Conrad. One, two, three, four, five …

Jason (*into his machine, likewise*) Testing! Gale Gilchrist. One, two, three, four, five …

Both of them rewind and replay their respective recorders. Satisfied, they switch back to "record" and place the machines on the table. Charlie is mildly amused by all this

Gale See how we all look out for you, Charlie. I hope you're appreciating all this.

Charlie (*cheerfully*) Thanks very much.

Gale I must say, meeting you for the first time, in person, looking at you sitting there, Charlie, it doesn't appear that any of this has really affected you. You still seem to me very modest, extremely unassuming ...

Charlie (*modestly unassuming*) Well ...

Jason He is. He's the most modest person you're ever likely to meet, Gale. Only he's too modest to say so himself. But I can tell you that over the eight years I've known him, he's hardly changed at all.

Gale Yes, that's where I'd like to start it. At the point when you first caught the public's imagination, Charlie. I mean, you appreciate it's a thirty-minute slot, we can't possibly cover everything. I think early years, all that sort of thing, we'll just touch on that, it's all on file, it's no problem. So we'll start with — where should we begin?

Jason *Breaking Point?*

Charlie *Breaking Point*, yes.

Gale This was the famous quiz show, of course?

Charlie Right.

Gale In which — just confirm this for me — you scored literally no points at all?

Jason Not a single point. It was a record.

Charlie I panicked, you know, that was the problem. I did fine in the trials, but ——

Jason But when he got in front of the cameras during the actual recording, he just froze up.

Charlie I froze up.

Gale But some of the questions — I dug the tape out and replayed it the other day — they were incredibly simple questions, some of them, weren't they?

Charlie I knew the answers. I knew the answers in my head. I just couldn't think of them.

Gale But in the end, of course, all that turned out in your favour?

Charlie I came last, certainly.

Gale But the personal fan mail afterwards was remarkable, wasn't it? That's the point.

Charlie Millions of letters. Emails. Faxes. I couldn't answer them all.

Jason He'd caught the public's imagination, you see ...

Gale And what did the people who won think about that, I wonder?

Charlie They weren't very pleased.

Jason They were a boring lot of people. They were just general public ...

Gale And shortly after that came your first big break with *Sports Quest*?

Charlie Right.

Jason Yes, their ratings were dropping, you see, and I offered them Charlie. They'd seen what happened on *Breaking Point* so they took a chance on him.

Gale Which they never regretted?
Jason Which they certainly never regretted.
Gale And you did that for —— ?
Jason Two years.
Charlie Two years. First six weeks as a regular panellist …
Gale Still getting things wrong?
Charlie … Mostly. Then I took over as question master ——
Jason — then he kept getting the questions wrong instead …
Gale But what I can't understand is why — (*She breaks off*)

Marsha enters. She is now dressed in her full Mr Chortles the Clown outfit: vivid make-up, false nose, fright wig and loud clothes, complete with big shoes and baggy trousers. The others watch as she passes. She has adopted her alternative persona, which is far more aggressive and outgoing than the timid woman we saw earlier

Oh, my God!
Charlie Good luck, then!

Marsha reacts by rushing at Charlie, feinting as if to attack him, running into an imaginary glass wall and knocking herself flat on her back. As she sits, a motor horn stitched into the seat of her trousers honks loudly. She leaps up, alarmed, twisting, trying to locate the source of the sound. She beats the seat of her trousers, causing the horn to sound again. This makes her rush off in panic, the horn sounding several more times as she goes

Gale (*after a pause to digest this*) Friend of yours, I take it?
Jason She's here to entertain the kids.
Gale Yes. Anyway. Of course, going back even further, even before *Breaking Point*, you started out wanting to be an athlete, didn't you? A runner?
Charlie Middle-distance, yes. I was a keen club runner.
Gale But that was quite eventful, too, wasn't it?
Charlie Yes, I was lucky enough to get picked for this friendly in Helsinki. And as a result of that ——
Jason Charlie had the potential in those days to be one of the finest middle-distance runners this country ever produced.
Gale But you only competed internationally just that once, right?
Charlie Yes, well, I broke down, of course.
Gale And never managed to finish?
Charlie No, I dropped out on the first bend. My knee went. You could hear it from the back of the stadium.
Jason Laid up for nearly a year.
Gale But you're all right now?

Charlie Oh, I'm all right now. As long as I don't run too far.

Jason That's when I first spotted Charlie, incidentally. I was watching that
particular international on TV and I said to myself then, that lad's got
something. Something special, out of the ordinary.

Gale Not as a runner, surely?

Jason No, not after that. He couldn't even walk. But what he did have, by
the bucketful, Gale, was charisma. Pure charm. I could spot that straight
away. And, I tell you, that's worth more than anything. I mean, plenty of
sportsmen — athletes — are talented. There's loads of them with ability.
But when it comes down to it, you know, sport isn't just about winning,
Gale.

Gale (*moving the recording machine to favour Jason*) It isn't?

Jason Not these days. There was a time before TV, before the mass media,
before the cameras were there, like, before they could get in really close and
pick up on the charisma of an individual, in those days all they had to rely
on was their own natural physical prowess. But then along came the new
brand of athlete — the sports personality like Charlie here — and the whole
scene was transformed for ever. And I was lucky enough to spot this early,
so when Linzi, who was another of my clients, introduced us, I took Charlie
on, no hesitation. And the rest is history, as they say.

Gale So as a sportsman, Charlie never won anything?

Charlie Not at international level, no. (*He smiles throughout the following*)

Gale Let's face it, he's never won anything at any level, has he?

Jason He doesn't need to win, Gale. That's the point. People like Charlie
supersede all that. The public no longer wants to sit and watch winners.
They're saturated with winners. Glutted. Winners? Come on, face it,
they're ten a penny. Anyone can win these days if they put their mind to
it. But what the Charlies of this world have, is something unique in
themselves, something they were born with. And the unique thing about
Charlie — sorry, Charlie, I'll let you get a word out in a minute — the
unique thing about Charlie is he has this ability to cross barriers. He knows
no boundaries. Anything he puts his hand to, he succeeds with.

Gale You mean he's no good at anything?

Jason No, no, no, Gale, you're missing the point ...

Gale Surely what you're saying is he's successful because he's a failure?

Jason ... no, you're missing the point.

Gale Then what?

Jason Ask the public, Gale. Don't ask me, ask the public.

*A pause. A children's cheer is heard in the distance. Chortles the Clown has
begun his routine. They look towards the garden, Gale frowning, momentarily
distracted*

Gale (*taking a breath*) Let me put the question another way. Charlie ...

Charlie What?

Gale What do you personally think it is about you? Do you sense it's because you invariably lose all the time? Is that what makes you so popular? Or is it all down to your personality?

Jason He's hardly the one to answer that, is he?

Gale Well, let him try. I mean, do you think if you won all the time, rather than lost, you'd have been so popular, Charlie?

Charlie (*shrugging*) No idea.

Jason I've said, it's not about winning …

Gale And, following on from that, have you ever, Charlie, with anything you've done, be honest, ever consciously tried to lose?

Charlie No. I always try my best. I always do.

Gale Maybe even *unconsciously* do you think you've ever tried to lose?

Charlie How do you mean?

Jason If he was unconscious, he wouldn't know about it, would he?

Gale No, seriously, listen. Most of us are conditioned to succeed in life, aren't we? One way or another. Right? Some of it's social pressure, school, parents, but some of it is surely genetic. We're born competitors, most of us. Most humans are instinctively competitive. Certainly men are. We try to succeed, to win. It's natural. Because when we win, we feel good about ourselves and, more important, it also attracts the esteem of others. Admiration. Popularity. Fame. Celebrity. And that way we feel loved. Respected. And conversely, when we lose — we feel bad about ourselves. Now the pressure on you, Charlie, seems to be to lose.

Charlie There's no pressure.

Gale Are you sure? I mean, watching some of those recordings of, say, *Sports Quest* — it's hard to believe that you didn't occasionally deliberately give a wrong answer.

Charlie I didn't.

Gale Never?

Charlie Why would I do that?

Jason You're asking him the wrong questions, Gale.

Gale What I'm asking is, do you fail, Charlie, because that's what people have come to expect of you? Thereby wanting to please them? For the same reason many of us need to succeed to gain approval, do you feel you need to fail to gain approval?

Charlie I think you're just complicating things, Gale. I'm just rubbish at everything, that's all.

Gale And does it make you feel good about yourself? I sense that it does.

Charlie Not really. I'm used to it. I'm useless. It doesn't bother me. I'm used to being useless. I was a useless baby.

Gale But, listen, lots of us fail. Most of us fail sometimes. Some of us fail a lot of the time. But we don't normally feel good about it, do we? We may pretend, stiff upper lip and all that, but we don't fool anyone. Other people don't rush up to congratulate us when we fail. They look pitying, or they pat us sympathetically on the back, or they simply avoid us. Give us time to lick our wounds, get over our shame. Whereas Charlie here, when he loses, he gets mobbed and swamped with fan mail. Why is that? Why? Tell me? For one thing, it's totally unfair on the rest of us, surely? Isn't it? On the winners?

Silence. Another cheer from the garden

Charlie I don't think I can help you, really. I'm sorry.

Gale (*rather wearily*) What I'm trying to establish, Charlie, is what it is that makes thousands of people — millions — tune in to watch you, turn up in their droves whenever you make a personal appearance or open a super-market? What is it about you?

Charlie Masses of people open supermarkets.

Gale Yes, but most of them have done something. You've never done anything, have you? It can't be because they all feel better than you, can it? Superior? Because in that case the normal reaction, surely, would be to despise you.

Charlie (*amused*) Despise me?

Gale It's the more normal human reaction.

Jason Come on, look at him. How could you despise that?

Charlie smiles at Gale. Gale is getting quite angry and frustrated underneath

Gale I feel like I did when I walked into your tunnel just now. You have the distinct impression you're climbing, that you're getting somewhere, only you finish up in exactly the same place you started.

Silence. Another cheer from the garden

Charlie (*shrugging*) Well.

Jason This is not the line you intend taking in the actual interview, is it?

Gale Probably not.

Jason Because you'll be wasting your breath.

Gale It's just I can't quite believe that you're for real, Charlie. I really can't.

Charlie (*smiling*) I feel real enough, Gale.

Jason's mobile rings

Jason Excuse me. (*Checking his phone*) Oh, it's Monty, I'd better take it, Charlie.

Charlie Sure.

Jason (*moving away, to Gale*) It's this new sponsorship, there's been a crossed line somewhere. (*Into the phone*) Hallo, Monty. ... how's it going, mate? ... Yes, beautiful. ... how's it with you? ... (*Laughing*) No, I don't believe it. ... Snow? ... you're joking. ... you are joking. ...

Jason goes off to the house

Gale and Charlie, alone, continue to stare at each other. Gale slips off her jacket. Charlie studies her

Gale They warned me you'd be like this.
Charlie Who did?
Gale The people I talked to about you. He's every interviewer's nightmare, they said. Charlie Conrad. Bland and impenetrable.
Charlie Bland? That's not very nice.
Gale I've watched the tapes. I've heard the recordings. I've read the cuttings. Journalists, interviewers, the best of them. The cream. All banging their heads against a brick wall.

Charlie shrugs

What makes you angry, Charlie? Do you ever get angry?
Charlie Yes, I get angry sometimes.
Gale And what makes you angry? What arouses your passions, Charlie?

Charlie considers

Gale Anything?
Charlie Cruelty to children.
Gale Good. Obvious, but good.
Charlie Cruelty to animals.
Gale Ditto.
Charlie Inconsiderate drivers on motorways.
Gale Mmmm ... Not right at the top of my list, but OK. What else?

There is a slight pause

Charlie Clever lady interviewers with an agenda who sit there trying to provoke me.
Gale (*sensing some sort of breakthrough*) Is that what I'm doing? Am I making you angry, Charlie?

Charlie reaches over and switches off Gale's recording machine

Charlie (*smiling*) I've watched your tapes as well. Seen your show, live. That's the way you work, isn't it? Wind people up. Try to get them to say things they don't mean to say.

Gale (*smiling too*) I have got through to you, then? You're not totally impenetrable?

Charlie I never said I was. What about you then, Gale? Would you describe yourself as impenetrable?

Gale, in turn, reaches over and switches off Jason's recording machine

Gale (*smiling*) Not at all. I'm penetrable, Charlie. Given the right circumstances, I'm perfectly penetrable.

Charlie That's good to hear.

Gale Mind you, it has to be two-way.

Charlie Naturally.

Gale Give a little, take a little. Give a little.

Charlie rises. He moves to Gale. She remains seated, staring up at him. Charlie bends down to her as if to kiss her. Gale puts up a hand gently to stop him

Just a bit public, don't you think?

Charlie smiles and moves to an archway at the back of the Tower, the one leading up. He stands at the entrance at the foot of the stairs, and looks at Gale. In a moment, Gale rises. Charlie watches her. Gale moves instead to the other archway, to the top of the stairs leading down. Charlie looks puzzled

(*Smiling*) Tell you what, I'll meet you halfway, shall I?

Charlie (*smiling*) Right.

In a moment, they both exit through their respective arches

The stage is empty for a second or so

Then Gale returns from the way she went and, moving to the table, gathers up her bag, jacket and recorder. She gives a final amused glance back at the archways, shakes her head and then makes to go off in the direction of the house

Before Gale can exit, though, Jason returns from the same direction, having finished his phone call

Jason Oh. All on your own?
Gale Yes.
Jason Where's Charlie gone?
Gale I — think he had an urgent call of nature.
Jason (*gathering up his own recorder from the table*) Oh, right. Well, do you fancy a stroll down, join the party for a bit?
Gale Why not?

They head towards the garden

Jason (*as they go*) Never know your luck, if we ask the grown-ups nicely there might even be some alcohol …
Gale Not for me …

Jason and Gale go off towards the garden

The stage remains empty for a moment. From the garden comes a final loud cheering and applause. Apparently Marsha has just finished her act

Charlie enters from the other archway having made the whole round trip. He looks puzzled at having failed to meet Gale

Charlie (*moving to the other archway, calling*) Gale! (*He moves to the table and sees that Gale's stuff has gone. He stands, restless and unhappy. He looks once more up at the house and down towards the garden. Reluctant to go in either direction, he goes back into the Tower*)

Oh, shit!

Marsha comes on, running. She is still in her full clown's costume. She is evidently quite breathless after her performance. She stands bent double, catching her breath

Neither Charlie nor Marsha see each other initially. Marsha throws herself down on the grass to rest a moment. The motor horn in her costume sounds. Charlie reacts. He watches Marsha. Marsha becomes aware she is not alone. She looks up and sees Charlie

Marsha (*starting to get to her feet*) Oh …
Charlie It's OK. Get your breath.
Marsha (*remaining seated*) I didn't … I'm sorry, I didn't see … Sorry.
Charlie (*kindly*) It's OK. Did your show go well?

Marsha Yes, they seemed to ... the children seemed to ... Lively. But good, good. Yes. Sorry, I'm still a bit ... Mr Chortles. You know. Always takes me a minute or two. I think your little boy — Harry — he really had a good time. He's lovely, isn't he? Looks terribly like you.

Charlie Yes ...

Marsha Mind you, I expect he's always being told that. You always hate that as a child, don't you? Continually being told you're like someone? When all you really want to look like is like yourself, don't you? I was always being told I looked like my mother. All the time. Constantly. I used to hate that. And now I'm nearly the age she was then, God, I actually do! Some days I look exactly like my mother. I mean, not now, obviously — like this — but normally. Sorry I'm ... rabbiting ... on ...

A silence

Did you — do you resemble either of your parents? I mean, did people ever say you did?

Charlie does not reply

Sorry ... I ... sorry ... None of my business.

Silence. During the following, Charlie sits on one of the chairs by the table

Charlie Tell me, when you entertain children, like you've just done, do you get great satisfaction from that?

Marsha Me? Well. It's complicated. You see, when I perform, I'm really not me, I become Mr Chortles, you see — I was trying to explain to your wife — to Linzi — but Mr Chortles certainly gets satisfaction, I know he does. It's just so rewarding hearing the children laughing and ——

Charlie Yes, but the point is, do you — do you — sorry, I don't know your name ——

Marsha Marsha.

Charlie Marsha. Do you, Marsha, get satisfaction? When you do a show? A performance?

Marsha Oh, yes. It's less direct, but yes. A sort of — afterglow. You know. When it's gone well. I expect like all of us, really. Whatever job you do. I was talking to a plumber once, you know, and he told me that whenever he installed a new central-heating system, there was always something so satisfying, so exciting, turning it all on for the first time and hearing all the water gushing round the pipes. You know, I expect sometimes he got leaks, but when he didn't ... I expect we're all like that really. When we've done something well. No leaks, you know. I'm sure it's like that with you, isn't it? It must be. Surely?

Charlie No.

Pause

I mean, up till now, I don't think it ever really bothered me. I've lived a sort of charmed life, you see. The less I succeeded, the more successful I became. When I ran that first race — that last race — I came tearing round this bend and I felt it go, my knee — I heard it go — and, I thought, that's it. That's the end of it. My chance ever to be famous. My one moment to be remembered. Gone for ever. And I lay there by the side of the track, you know — and the pain was unbelievable — I was nearly fainting with the pain — and then as they were lifting me on the stretcher, all I could hear — through the pain — was the cheering. People shouting and cheering. And I thought it's that bloody Finn, isn't it? He's won again, the bastard. But then, as they were carrying me down the tunnel to the dressing room, you know, this cheering just kept on and on, getting louder and louder and I thought, they're not cheering for him at all, the Finn, they're cheering me, for God's sake. And then came all these journalists and TV crews, all wanting to talk to me. How did it feel? Can you describe your disappointment …? Are you at all bitter? And I said, no, not really, only with my parents. I'm bitter with my parents that they couldn't provide me with a better set of knees, that's all. But apart from that … No, I couldn't understand it. I became a national hero. I mean, the bloke who won the race, he hardly got a mention. Went home alone on the bus, probably. And it's been the same ever since. Quiz programmes, panel shows — and the more I bugger them up … I opened this supermarket the other day, knocked a whole bloody display stand over. Twelve foot high mountain of beans cascading all over the place, down the aisles and that. Nearly killed the manager. They didn't seem to mind. Booked me to open seven more branches. Paying me a fortune. And then I see someone like you with genuine talent, which I'm sure you have, and I think ... where's the justice? Eh?

Silence. Marsha watches him

The trouble is it's — it's into my personal life as well. My marriage is — well, slipping away. I know it is. Linzi — my wife's — disappointed, I think. Unhappy, anyway. I can understand that. She had talent, too. Real talent. But, I ask you, what's the point of having real talent — when someone like me comes along? Makes a mockery of it? And then just now — I nearly did something so crass — so stupid — it was like taking a box of matches and setting fire to my life — it was that stupid. And I would have done it. If she'd — if she hadn't … That's the terrible thing. Sometimes, you don't need to have done something. It's knowing that you could easily

have done something—it's just as bad, isn't it? I mean in my mind, I really
wanted … Gets you sometimes, doesn't it? Sorry. (*He looks at Marsha*)
And there you are, sitting there, listening to me bleating on about my
miserable life. Saying to yourself, what's this sad git complaining about?
Bloody great house, beautiful wife, two gorgeous kids, eight figure income
or whatever … I don't even know, I've stopped counting. Fame, fortune,
celebrity. You name it. What more does he want? Why doesn't he just shut
up and enjoy it? And, you know, I could, I really could. If someone would
give me one reason, one solitary good reason, why I deserve any of it.

*A silence. Marsha rises, slips off her outsized shoes and moves to where
Charlie is sitting. She steps on to the table and, from somewhere within her
costume, produces a prop flower. She offers it to Charlie. He takes it,
bemused. She steps down, so she is close to him*

Marsha (*softly*) I think you're wonderful. You changed my life. I used to
    think I was nothing. Then I saw you and I thought, no. You don't have to
    be anything to be something.

Charlie rises, staring at her

Marsha Have you — ? Have you got a pen?
Charlie (*dully*) A what?
Marsha A pen. You promised to give me an autograph.
Charlie Oh, yes. Of course. (*He turns away, fumbling in his pocket to find
    a pen*)

*Marsha slips the braces off her shoulders and allows her trousers to drop to
her ankles. Underneath, she is wearing clown-like, long frilly bloomers*

    Sorry, I haven't got a piece of — Have you got any … ?
Marsha My thigh. Could you sign my thigh?
Charlie (*turning to see her, startled*) Your what?
Marsha (*pulling up one bloomer leg, urgently*) My thigh. Here. Sign my
    thigh! Please sign my thigh! Sign my thigh!
Charlie Oh, for God's sake!
Marsha (*louder, imploringly*) Please! Please!
Charlie All right! All right! I'll sign your thigh! Here! (*He moves to her and
    makes as if to sign the outside of her thigh*)

*Marsha immediately lies on the table and, parting her legs slightly, indicates
her inner leg*

Marsha No, no, not there. Here! Here! On the inside …
Charlie What?
Marsha (*louder still, agitatedly*) Please, please, please … Inside! *Inside!*
Charlie (*becoming equally agitated*) All right! All right! All right!

Charlie tries to sign the inside of Marsha's leg but things get out of hand. Marsha, removing her clown's nose, aims a badly directed kiss at Charlie. Charlie responds. The pen and the flower go flying and they are both wrestling together on the table

  (*Disbelievingly*) Oh, my God! I don't believe this!
Marsha Yes, yes, yes, yes, yes!

Charlie starts the serious business of removing Marsha's comedy bloomers (underneath she wears rather more conventional underwear). Throughout all this, the motor horn sewn into her trousers continues to sound from time to time as Charlie steps on it

Charlie Wait! Wait! What am I doing?
Marsha Please, please, please!

Charlie succeeds in removing the bloomers

  Linzi enters from the garden. She is leading by the hand the two little girls, Laura and Katie, both of whom are now dressed in home-made fancy dress bride's outfits. Behind her come Jason and Gale

Linzi (*as she enters*) Guess who won the fancy dress, then! We did! Yes! Here, I've brought our two little brides to —— (*She stops as she witnesses the scene*)

  She swiftly turns both girls away to protect them from the fearful sight and rushes them back into the garden. Gale and Jason part to allow them to exit

Charlie stands, still holding the bloomers

Marsha rises with a cry of alarm. She pulls up her trousers protectively and with another cry rushes off through the archway at the back. Her sobs and footsteps recede

Charlie instinctively moves after her to return her undergarment, but she is gone. Silence. Charlie stands rather sheepishly, still holding the bloomers. The other two stare at him, Gale amused, Jason in some state of shock

A moment and then Marsha's cries are heard coming towards us from the other archway. Charlie turns

   Marsha emerges through the second archway and stops, momentarily bemused at seeing Charlie and the others again

Marsha (*breathlessly*) Help! Please help me, I — ! I'm — !

Charlie makes a fresh attempt to offer her the bloomers

   Marsha realises who she's appealing to, screams once more and rushes back the way she's just come

   (*Echoing, off*) Aaaaaahhhhhhh!

Silence

Charlie (*at length, waving the bloomers by way of explanation*) I was — just giving her an autograph.

As he stands there, we hear Marsha's cries approaching again from the original archway

   (*Turning back towards the archway somewhat wearily, realizing this could be a lengthy procedure*) Oh, no …

Before Marsha can re-emerge yet again —

The Lights fade to Black-out

C<small>URTAIN</small>

ACT II
SCENE 1

The same. A few weeks later; a fine day in August

When the CURTAIN *rises the garden is lit with bright summer sunshine*

Hugo de Préscourt QC, a very smart, expensive barrister in his forties, is waiting, somewhat impatiently

After a moment, Jason and Charlie come from the house. Both look concerned

Jason Hallo, Hugo. Here we are, mate!

Hugo Jason! Charlie! How are you both? Good to see you.

Charlie Hugo.

Hugo Hallo, Charlie. So sorry to hear about all this, old chum.

Charlie Yes, well …

Hugo How's Linzi? Bearing up, is she?

Charlie Yes, she's bearing up.

Hugo That's the spirit, that's my girl! How's Judy these days, Jason?

Jason Oh, she's OK. Thank you for asking, Hugo. Apologies. We got delayed. Something came up.

Hugo Yes. They'll be here very shortly. I really do need a word with you both before they come. Put you in the full picture. (*Noticing their manner*) What is it? Problems?

Jason Another one's pulled out. Another sponsor.

Hugo Ah.

Jason That's the third in four days. The major one this time.

Hugo Oh dear, that's bad. Look, sit down, both of you. We do need to chat.

Jason and Charlie sit

I have to be honest with you, chummies, there's only a limited amount of damage limitation I can possibly manage. The problem is, Charlie, that whatever you did — and I won't go into what you did or didn't do ——

Charlie I didn't do anything, I keep saying ——

Hugo Wait! Wait! Wait! Let me finish! Whatever you did, you unfortunately chose to do in front of a highly influential member of our beloved mass media. So there's no chance of getting this hushed up. No chance.

However, all is not lost, there is a certain amount I can do and please rest assured that I will do it. The first thing is to keep this out of court, of course. If it reaches the courts then we might as well take out an advert on the side of a number nineteen bus. Now, as far as I can gather, they're claiming on their side, sexual intimidation, indecent assault ——

Charlie What?

Hugo They've stopped short of rape, thankfully, because that would be much more serious ——

Charlie No way!

Hugo Nonetheless, this is something we do need to boot very, very firmly into touch. Fortunately, I do know Diggs, I've had dealings with him before ——

Jason Who?

Hugo Simeon Diggs, the girl's solicitor. We've met before. He's — he's a nice enough chap but not essentially from the top drawer if you follow me. Tends to push his case far too hard. First-class chap with a second-class brain, if you follow me. Still, we mustn't underestimate him.

Charlie Listen, he doesn't even have a case ——

Hugo Prima facie, Charlie, prima facie, they do ——

Charlie Prima bollocks!

Jason Easy, Charlie, easy, lad!

Hugo Charlie, listen to me. You're both of you discovered alone, the woman's lying flat on her back screaming while you're standing over her ripping off her how's-your-fathers. Now that's not good, Charlie, I'd hate to go before a jury with that one, I really would.

Charlie I was giving the woman an autograph! She wanted my autograph!

There is a slight pause

Hugo Yes, well, enough said. I don't think we'll venture any further down that particular alley. The important thing is, we've got them both to agree to come here today which I have to say took a hell of a lot of doing. The task now is to ensure we blow them and their wretched little case clean out of the pond. OK? Now, at the end of the day, when stumps are drawn, this may entail slipping them a back-hander, I can't rule that out altogether …

Charlie Oh, for God's sake!

Hugo Charlie, old chum, believe me, anything's better than the alternative.

Charlie What's the point of giving them money? The damage is done, isn't it? Sponsors cancelling, programmes being shelved, I mean, what is this? I'm being branded a serial rapist or whatever without even having a chance to defend myself.

Hugo Well, that's the dear old general public for you, isn't it?

Charlie It's not the dear old general public at all, it's the dear old bloody newspapers …

Hugo Now come on, you can't blame the papers, they're only reflecting public opinion, that's all they're doing …

Charlie (*agitatedly*) What are you talking about? The public didn't have an opinion till the papers gave them one … No one's even asked me for my version.

Hugo (*soothingly*) All right, Charlie! Charlie! Charlie! I'm on your side, chummy. I'm listening. OK? I'm listening to you. OK?

Charlie OK.

Hugo All right then. Now, what's your version? Calmly. Go on. Tell me in your own words

Charlie (*trying to be calmer*) She came up to me and she said, can I have your autograph? And I said, yes, of course. And she said, have you got a pen? And I said, yes. And then I said, have you got a bit of paper? And she said, no, she hadn't, but could I sign her thigh?

Hugo Sign her thigh.

Charlie Right.

Hugo And — er — sorry to interrupt, Charlie, but that's standard procedure is it, to sign thighs, is it? Do you sign many women's thighs?

Charlie No. Not normally, no. Hands, sometimes. Arms. Legs occasionally. I've signed an occasional shoulder.

Hugo Right, right. But a thigh you'd consider an unusual request?

Charlie Yes, quite unusual.

Hugo So the first question I'm bound to ask, Charlie, is why? Why agree to a thigh? Why a thigh?

Charlie Well, I was trying to — trying to be obliging. She was quite anxious.

Hugo Nonetheless fairly risky, don't you think, Charlie? I mean, perilously close, isn't it? A thigh. Within a whisker's breadth of a major erogenous zone.

Charlie Yes, but I was going to sign the outside.

Hugo The outside?

Charlie Just below her hip.

Hugo I see.

Charlie Only she suddenly twists around, you know, and — you know, spreads them slightly — her legs — and says she wants it inside.

Hugo Wants what inside?

Charlie She wants signing inside, you know. On her inside leg. Instead.

Hugo I see. That was a bit cheeky of her, wasn't it? So what did you say?

Charlie Well, I was — I was all for signing her but then she goes wild, she tries to kiss me — and things got out of hand.

Hugo And at what stage, Charlie, think about this most carefully before you answer — at what stage did you remove her — take down her you-know-whats?

Charlie Well, I ——

Hugo Because they're bound to bring this up, you know that.

Charlie Yes, well, after that.

Hugo After the first attempted kiss by her?

Charlie Yes.

Hugo Now you see, we're already wading into deep do-do here, Charlie. You freely admit that after she kissed you, things got out of hand — your words, Charlie — that you abandoned the idea of signing an autograph but nonetheless went ahead and started removing her undergarments. Removing them, I may add, with some force. There is, apparently, damage to the — to the aforesaids. (*Shaking his head*) I'm sorry, but if we ran with that, Charlie, old chum, you'd have less chance than a prize pig in a bacon-slicer. You'd probably go down for ten years.

Charlie But she wanted it — she begged me.

Hugo (*wagging a cautionary finger*) Ah! Ah! Ah! I beseech you, don't even think about going there, old boy.

Charlie How do you mean?

Hugo Her word against yours, old lad. Fatal. Unless she turns up in court in fishnet tights, nine-inch heels and a beret, they'll inevitably take her side against yours, they always do.

Charlie Even if she's mad?

Hugo (*momentarily interested*) Ah. You think she may be mad, do you?

Charlie I think she's peculiar.

Hugo Well, ninety per cent of women are peculiar, I don't think we can try that one. No, no. You see, if we offer them your version, they're bound to try to discredit it. But if we don't offer them a version, there's nothing for them to discredit, is there? On the other hand, since they're in the role of the plaintiff, as it were, they're honour-bound to offer us their version. Her version. Which we can then discredit. We discredit her version entirely and then later on we offer them a nice little sum by way of compensation and they toddle off satisfied into the sunset.

Charlie Except I'm — what? — five thousand quid worse off or something.

Hugo (*doubtfully*) I think we'll be lucky to get away with that. Even with Simeon Diggs.

Charlie (*resigned*) Whatever.

Jason Listen, this is all very well, but what's going to happen in the long term? I mean, even if we do discredit her, all this is very damaging to Charlie. We're losing accounts, we're losing contracts, we've just lost our main sponsor — we're losing friends …

Hugo Yes. Well, it's all got very emotive overtones, I'm afraid. *In flagrante* with a clown, for heaven's sake! Couldn't you at least have chosen a tightrope-walker? Children's clown. Note those two words carefully, chummies. Dynamite. Children. Clown. Little eager faces, shining, expectant. A simple, innocent, laughing, child-like clown ——

Charlie She's thirty years old.

Hugo And if that wasn't enough, two young children from next door, both dressed in white, in their nauseating little bride's outfits, witnessing at first hand their beloved clown who so recently entertained them, being stripped and ravished in front of their very eyes by a TV personality they had been taught to adore and to trust. Frankly, I'm expecting a suit from the mother any day now. No, they'll make what they choose to make of it, Charlie. Nothing we can do to stop them, I'm afraid. Unfortunately, the fact is you are due for a fall really, aren't you? It's a terrible thing to say but, let's face it, this chap here's had seven good years, hasn't he, Jason? That's a very long time in the media spotlight, Charlie, old chum. Jolly good! You've done frightfully well really, haven't you? But I think you're just going to have to tighten the belt now, old boy, and prepare like the old Pharaoh for at least seven lean years.

Charlie I keep saying, I didn't do anything.

Hugo OK. Let me ask you this. One last question. Just between us. Let's accept for a second that you didn't do anything. But did you *intend* anything? Search your heart and tell me, what was your intention, Charlie?

Charlie is silent. Hugo sits. A moment

(*At length*) Of course, it would all be a lot simpler if that bloody television woman hadn't witnessed it all.

Jason Well, she's on the way out, anyway.

Hugo Who? Gale Gilchrist? Really?

Jason I heard yesterday. On the grapevine. They're axing her programme.

Hugo Really?

Jason Apparently. Her lover got caught in a drugs bust. Dealing and all. Gale could be implicated.

Hugo Who's the lover?

Jason — er — Melanie. Melanie Messina. You know, the one that does that afternoon kids' programme. What's it called? *Skippitydoodah!*

Charlie reacts

Hugo Don't know it. Not a regular viewer, I'm afraid.

Jason Hey, Charlie, just occurred to me, there's an opening for Linzi there, isn't there? She wants to get back in, doesn't she? I'll put in a word with those Toybox people. Melanie Messina won't be dancing round in a romper suit any more, that's for sure. Not in Holloway. Not if she's got any sense. (*Producing a notebook*) I'll make a note of that. (*He writes*)

Charlie (*still stunned*) I didn't know Gale Gilchrist was gay?

Jason Didn't you? I thought everyone knew that.

Hugo I don't see that much television these days. I only watch the news, occasionally. And then only if I'm on. (*He laughs*)

Silence

Jason Anyway, Gale's on her way out. She won't be a problem much longer.
Hugo Journalists are always a problem, chummy. They're like snakes, journalists. They don't stop rattling till you cut their bloody heads off. (*Looking at his watch*) Where have these wretched people got to, then?
Jason Maybe stuck on the motorway.
Hugo Well, we all managed to get here, didn't we?
Jason You were all right, you came in a helicopter.
Hugo Time is money. I was only trying to save you money, old chum.

From the house, Linzi appears. She has changed her hair colour dramatically and is pale and tense. She is followed by Marsha and Simeon. Marsha is now dressed in a plain, demure outfit as befits a wronged party. She holds back slightly during the following. Simeon, her solicitor, about the same age as Hugo, is a rather downmarket version of him, dressed in a somewhat shiny, off-the-peg suit

Hugo rises, at once the genial, welcoming host. Charlie and Jason follow suit

Aha! Aha! Here they all are! Welcome! Welcome! (*Embracing Linzi*) Hallo, Linzi darling, how lovely to see you.
Linzi (*flatly*) Hallo, Hugo.
Hugo My God, you're looking wonderful, darling. Wonderful! Tell me, you've done something to your hair, haven't you?
Linzi (*touching her hair vaguely*) Possibly. (*Indicating Simeon*) Do you know Mr ... ? Mr Diggs, is it?
Hugo Of course I know Mr Diggs. (*Wringing Simeon's hand, overjoyed*) Diggsy, my dear chap, lovely to see you, old chum.
Simeon (*a little overwhelmed by the warmth of this welcome*) Hallo, Hugo ...
Hugo I have to tell you all that Diggsy here and I — we go back — well, literally forever. School chums, weren't we? Bosom school chums?
Simeon We were at school together, yes.
Hugo Now, Simeon, have you met my client, Charlie Conrad? Give yourself a treat and meet Charlie Conrad.
Simeon No. I haven't had the pleasure. I know of you, of course. See you often enough on television. Simeon Diggs.
Charlie (*nodding to Simeon*) Hallo.
Simeon My daughter's a great fan. So's my wife actually ...

Hugo (*laughing*) What woman isn't? Show me a woman who isn't in love with Charlie Conrad, eh?

They suddenly all become aware of Marsha. There is a slight pause. If Hugo is at all fazed by this he doesn't show it

Linzi (*coolly*) Can I offer anyone tea or coffee or anything?
Simeon (*somewhat hopefully*) Er ——
Hugo Please don't go to any trouble … None of us want coffee, do we?
Simeon No.
Linzi Sure? I must get on then. Excuse me. (*She moves away*)
Hugo You're looking an absolute picture, darling.
Linzi (*as she goes*) Thank you.

Linzi exits back to the house

Simeon May I introduce my client, Hugo? This is Miss Bates. Marsha Bates. Marsha, this is ——
Hugo (*stepping forward and taking Marsha's hand*) Hugo de Préscourt. Hallo, there, lovely to meet you, Miss Bates. Now do let's find you a chair, shall we?
Marsha (*mutedly*) Thank you.

During the following there is a general shuffling whilst Marsha is seated by Hugo and the men in turn then sit down. Simeon sits next to Marsha. Hugo manages to seat himself in a prime position near to Charlie, his back to the sun, causing Simeon and Marsha to squint at him with difficulty. Jason chooses to sit a little apart from the main group

Hugo (*busily organizing*) If you'd care to sit here, Miss Bates, I think that's the comfiest, and I expect you'll want to sit next to your client, Simeon …
Simeon Yes, I'll sit here …
Hugo Charlie, you here by me — and Jason — oh, you're OK there, are you? We've all met Jason, have we? Jason Ratcliffe, everyone?
Simeon Yes, hallo, I think we have met actually, haven't we?
Jason (*who can't remember*) Yes, very possibly.
Simeon Yes, I remember. How's your wife? How's Judy these days?
Jason Very well, kind of you to ask.
Simeon Send her my regards. Simeon Diggs. Remember me to her.
Jason I will.
Hugo Jason here is Charlie's agent — manager, Marsha. His what-have-you …
Jason … what-have-you …

They are now all seated

Hugo (*the genial host*) Now then, are we all sitting comfortably? I'd just like
to say, at the top, Simeon, how much we appreciate your both agreeing to
meet us like this. We do see it as a splendid gesture on your part.
Simeon As I said on the phone, Hugo, this is not our first choice of venue.
We would have far preferred it — Miss Bates — Marsha — would have
far preferred it, if we had met in rather more neutral, less painful
surroundings. In, say, an office ——
Hugo Absolutely. As I say, a terrific gesture, thank you so much, Miss Bates.
It was simply that between the three of us, Charlie, Jason and I, this was the
only way of getting us all together at once.
Simeon Yes, and we did try to accommodate your own busy ——
Hugo As I say, a very big thank you on behalf of us all, Simeon. It really is
appreciated.

Pause

(*More seriously*) Now then, to the business in hand. Simeon, we've been
having a chat, the three of us, very briefly just filling in time before you
arrived, and I think it would be fair to sum up our position as this. We're
aware your client, Miss Bates, has a complaint against my client, Mr
Conrad. And what we'd dearly love is to hear that complaint, in full. In her
own words. And then from there, let's see if we can't all somehow go
forward to come to an arrangement that would satisfy all parties. Without
the costly, time-consuming rigmarole of dragging it through the courts. Is
that a fair summing up? Charlie? Jason?

Jason and Charlie nod

Hugo Right. Now, we're all ears, Simeon, the floor is yours, old chum. (*He
leans back and looks at Simeon and Marsha expectantly*)
Simeon Well, I think the basic facts are quite simple and not in dispute.
The events were after all witnessed by several people, including
unfortunately a prominent member of the media and, more regrettably
still, by two small, impressionable under-aged children. Also of
course, until she rushed away in a state of shock, briefly by your client's
wife herself. The facts are these ——
Hugo Facts?
Simeon — the facts, according to Miss Bates, are these. Miss Bates —
Marsha — had concluded her performance before an audience of children
down in the garden there. She returned somewhat tired and exhausted and
on her way to her changing room — the downstairs — er — bathroom in

the hall there — she passed by this Tower where she chanced to see Mr Conrad. When they'd met a little earlier, Mr Conrad had promised Miss Bates his autograph. Miss Bates reminded him of his promise and Mr Conrad produced his pen. Unfortunately there being no convenient scrap of paper ready to hand, Mr Conrad suggested that perhaps he sign some portion of Miss Bates's anatomy instead. Miss Bates consented, albeit reluctantly, awed at finding herself alone in the presence of such a famous figure as Mr Conrad. However, alarm bells started to ring when Mr Conrad suggested that he sign Miss Bates's thigh rather than the more conventional arm, hand or even shoulder. Before she could object, Mr Conrad forced her to the ground and, to her horror, started forcibly to remove her undergarments despite her ensuing protests. Fortunately at this stage, the others arrived and Mr Conrad was forced to release my client who then fled in panic, still half-dressed and in fear and confusion. Those are the basic facts. I don't think I've left anything out, have I, Miss Bates?

Marsha (*in barely a whisper*) No.

Silence

Charlie Look, I can't sit here and listen to ——

Hugo gives Charlie a look. Charlie shuts up

Hugo Yes. Those are grave accusations, you know, Simeon chum, very grave accusations indeed.

Simeon They are. You don't dispute them, I trust?

Hugo Well, I — I do feel that your version of this ——

Simeon It's not our version, Hugo, they're the facts ——

Hugo — let's call it that for the present, shall we, just for the sake of argument ——? Your version. Your version really does raise far more questions than it answers, it really does. I mean, frankly, Simeon, we're all a bit perplexed by this, we really are. And as for Charlie here, well, as you can see, he's in a distressed state.

Simeon Maybe because he's ——

Hugo No, no, wait! Wait! You see, you talk about Miss Bates — Marsha, may I call you Marsha? — being confused. But what about poor old Charlie here? What do you think all this did to him?

Simeon What are you saying? Are you trying to imply that Mr Conrad was in some way the victim —— ?

Hugo Could I — may I have permission to ask Marsha here a couple of small questions? Would you object to that? Please?

Simeon Well ... (*To Marsha*) Would you mind? You don't have to, you know.

Marsha I don't mind.

Hugo Thank you, Marsha. (*Kindly*) Now, Marsha, I'm just trying to clear all this up, you know, for all our sakes. I'm not here to pressure you or bully you into saying something you don't mean. Heaven forbid. That's why Simeon's here, after all. To make sure I don't.

Simeon He certainly is.

Hugo Marsha, you're an entertainer, right?

Marsha Yes.

Hugo A children's entertainer?

Marsha Yes.

Hugo You're fond of children, I take it?

Marsha (*smiling a little*) Yes.

Hugo Well, let's face it, who isn't? Who could ever resist a smiling child? So you're a children's entertainer but quite an unusual one, I believe.

Marsha How do you mean?

Hugo Well, as far as I can gather, when you perform, you perform as a man, don't you? You adopt, if that's the word, a male persona? Is that right, Marsha? Have I got that right?

Marsha Yes.

Simeon Hugo, where is all this —— ?

Hugo Just a tick, just a tick. I let you have your say, old chum — So, Marsha, when you become this person — what's he called? Mr Chumbly, is it?

Marsha Mr Chortles …

Hugo Mr Chortles — what a wonderful name — (*he laughs*) — when you become this Mr Chortles, I understand he tends to take you over completely, doesn't he?

Marsha Just a little, yes …

Hugo No, not just a little, surely? I think completely. That's the word you've been known to use — completely, Marsha? Isn't that right?

Marsha Yes.

Hugo So, when you came up that hill there after your performance, hot and tired and exhausted, I imagine — the children's laughter still ringing in your ears — tell me how much of you at that point was Marsha and how much was still Mr Chortles?

Marsha I was — I was ——

Hugo I mean, you were still dressed as Mr Chortles, weren't you? You were, to all appearances, still male?

Marsha No, I was me, I was me —

Hugo But surely you'd gone to terrific trouble to make yourself look like a man, hadn't you? Large trousers, big boots, a funny wig … I mean, I didn't see it, but from all accounts you were pretty convincing. Managed to fool the best part of a hundred kids, didn't you? I mean, modesty aside, you're damned good, Marsha, aren't you? Admit it.

Marsha (*modestly*) Well …

Hugo In all that gear you can deceive most people, can't you? Including, and this is the acid test, isn't it, eagle-eyed children. I mean, none of them shouted out fraud, it's a girl! There's a beautiful girl under that lot! Did they?

Marsha (*smiling*) No.

Hugo No. Then how do you think Mr Conrad here could tell?

Marsha (*startled*) What?

Hugo Don't you feel he'd be just as confused?

Marsha (*slightly puzzled*) Well, he knew.

Hugo He knew what?

Marsha He knew it was me.

Hugo How did he know?

Marsha Because I told him.

Hugo You told him. You said to him, hallo, it's me, Marsha Bates under all this.

Marsha I didn't need to. He knew it was me. He'd promised me an autograph.

Hugo (*smiling*) Marsha, have you any idea how many autographs Mr Conrad here signs in your average day? Fifty? A hundred? About that, would you say, Charlie?

Charlie Usually.

Hugo Now, with respect, Marsha, how could he possibly be expected to remember one person in particular? As far as Charlie was concerned he was innocently signing an autograph for this Mr Chortles. Just another clown.

Simeon I don't know where this is all leading, Hugo. The fact is that, whoever he thought it was, the assault took place ——

Hugo (*pained*) Simeon, please. Please, allow me to finish, old chum. I'm so nearly there. So, Marsha, Charlie was under the impression that he was signing an autograph for a male fan, Mr Chortles. OK, so far?

Marsha But he wasn't, he knew it was me, he ——

Hugo Just for the sake of argument, let's agree he genuinely thought he was signing for this Mr Chortles … In law we have this phrase, Marsha. Shadow of doubt. Shadow of doubt. Marsha. So can we agree that? Just for a second. Because that was genuinely Mr Conrad's impression, I can assure you. That he was signing Mr Chortles. So then we come to the question, why? Why should he assault you?

Marsha I don't know ——

Hugo Marsha, looking at me, would you have guessed that I'm gay? That I'm a gay man?

Marsha (*a bit surprised*) No …

Hugo It's not something I'm in the least ashamed of. It's not something I make a secret of — except in certain courtrooms before certain judges — but normally, I'm an open book. Similarly with Mr Conrad, there. Would you have thought that Mr Conrad was gay?

Marsha He's not.

Hugo And you'd be right. He's not. Mr Conrad — sparing your blushes, Charlie — is as full-bloodedly heterosexual as any man has a decent right to expect. But the one thing he is not — and, believe me, I have known this man many years now, Marsha — the one thing Charlie Conrad would never consider, would be to lie down with another man for sexual purposes.

Simeon Oh, really, this is becoming absolutely ——

Hugo The idea would never have entered his head.

Marsha (*becoming agitated now*) Then why did he do it, then?

Hugo I suggest to you that he was merely trying to accede to a request for an autograph. An autograph that you requested. But when Mr Conrad innocently produced his pen you bared your thigh and insisted he sign it.

Marsha No ...

Hugo Exposing to him your inside leg and beseeching him, nay, begging him ——

Simeon Now, stop this at once ——

Marsha It was him! It was him!

Hugo Are you completely sure of that, Miss Bates?

Marsha Of course I am. Otherwise why did he pull off my underclothes? Ask him that!

Pause

Hugo (*more calmly*) Very well. I had hoped to avoid this but, very well let's talk about underclothes for a moment, shall we? Would you care to describe those underclothes, Miss Bates? The ones you allege Mr Conrad ripped from you?

Marsha They — were — long — multi-coloured — knee-length — frilly — you know ... elasticated ...

Hugo Go on.

Marsha They were just comedy bloomers, that's all.

Hugo Comedy bloomers? I see. I presume female comedy bloomers?

Marsha Yes, of course. Men don't normally wear — do they?

Hugo I have no idea. You tell me, Miss Bates. I may be gay but I have no first-hand experience of transvestism.

Marsha Well, they don't.

Hugo Then you would be amazed, would you not, to see, say, Mr Diggs wearing comedy bloomers?

Simeon What?

Hugo If Mr Diggs were to drop his trousers here and now, God forbid, would you be startled, even a little disturbed, were he found to be wearing comedy bloomers?

Marsha Of course.

Hugo Then what effect do you think it had on Mr Conrad? When Mr Chortles dropped his own trousers and revealed he was wearing them?

Marsha That was entirely different ——

Hugo How much more startled, how much more disturbed do you think Mr Conrad would be? A red-blooded male confronted by someone he assumed to be of similar sex wearing such a garment? Indignation, perhaps? Anger? Revulsion, even? Can you altogether forgive him for wishing to remove them, to tear away this insult to his manhood as fast as he possibly could?

Simeon This is ridiculous, we're talking about a pantomime garment here, how could anyone take offence?

Hugo Ah, would that it were merely pantomime, Diggsy. The innocence of pantomime. But, alas, it wasn't. Pantomime, surely, is at least consistent. At least it is honest cross-dressing. When the pantomime dame raises her skirts, there traditionally, as one would anticipate, are indeed comedy bloomers. In pantomime the principal boy, though a girl, remains strictly a boy, the dame, though a man, remains firmly female. But what are we to make of you, Miss Bates? Who chooses on the one hand to dress as a man and yet secretly cross-dresses back again as a woman?

Marsha That's nonsense ——

Hugo (*his voice growing louder*) What signals are we meant to interpret from that, Miss Bates?

Simeon Mr de Préscourt ——!

Hugo Do you even know the answer, Miss Bates?

Marsha Of course, I do ——

Hugo When you lie alone in bed at night, tell me, when your body cries out, which sex do you answer to, Miss Bates?

Simeon (*rising*) Mr de Préscourt ——!

Marsha (*becoming very distraught now*) I'm a woman!

Hugo Are you sure of that? Wouldn't you prefer I call you sir, Mr Chortles?

Marsha No, I'm a woman!

Simeon Mr de Préscourt ——!

Hugo (*fiercely*) Are you sure? In your heart, are you absolutely sure?

Marsha I'm a woman!

Hugo (*standing close to her now*) Tell me just what exactly are you? Do you even know?

Marsha, in great agitation, leaps to her feet and starts to pull at her clothing

Marsha (*shouting*) I'm a woman! I'm a woman! *I'm a woman! You see? Look!* (*She manages briefly to bare her top. She stands there defiantly*)

Hugo averts his gaze. Simeon swiftly removes his jacket and covers his client. Marsha collapses in his arms

Simeon This is outrageous, Hugo, absolutely outrageous.
Hugo My case rests, Mr Diggs.
Simeon I'll have you disbarred for this, I've never seen such behaviour!
Hugo I'll give you a bell in the morning, old chum.
Simeon (*gathering up Marsha's discarded clothes*) I'm reporting this, I warn you. I'll see you're disbarred, Hugo.
Hugo I feel sure we can come to some arrangement …
Simeon You always were a little bastard even at school. Look what you've done to this girl.
Marsha (*muffled, sobbing*) I'm a woman …
Simeon Don't you care? Don't you even care? Look at her, poor kid!
Marsha I'm a woman!

Simeon heads back towards the house with Marsha

Simeon Yes, all right, my dear! I'll drive you home! I'll take you home! Come on, poor little thing!
Marsha I'm a woman!
Simeon (*soothingly*) There! There! There!
Hugo I'll give you a bell.

Simeon goes off, supporting Marsha

Charlie and Jason still look a little stunned

Hugo I think that was all fairly satisfactory, don't you? He certainly won't risk her on the witness stand. Not after that. I'll come to some arrangement with him tomorrow, Charlie, once he's calmed down a bit. I'll try my best to keep it to five figures, promise. Jason, old chum, I wonder, would you mind awfully seeing them off?
Jason What?
Hugo Only I'd appreciate a quiet word with Charlie here, do you mind? Just before I take wing.
Jason Oh. Right. I'll see you later, Charlie.
Charlie Sure.
Jason Cheers, Hugo.

Hugo Cheer-ho, Jason. Lovely to see you, old chum. By the way, I've got
a spare ticket for the Lords Final, if you fancy that?
Jason Right, you're on.
Hugo I'll give you a bell. Love to the lovely Judy.

Jason exits

Hugo Thoroughly nice chap, isn't he? First-rate. You're lucky to have him.
Charlie I know.
Hugo Listen, Charlie, this is a bit awkward but — I didn't want to say this
in front of the others — but Linzi's asked me to start proceedings.
Charlie What?
Hugo Proceedings. Divorce proceedings.

Charlie sits down, stunned

Sorry, old chum. That come a bit out of the blue, did it?
Charlie (*incredulous*) Divorce?
Hugo I'm very sorry.
Charlie (*dully*) Why?
Hugo (*shrugging*) Who knows with marriage? Things run out of steam. The
relationship passes its sell-by date. Who knows? Anyway, Linzi feels she
needs to graze a fresh paddock, needs to get out from under. You know how
they get.
Charlie Is it because of — of what happened with ——
Hugo God, no. Heavens no. She's not going to divorce you over a pair of
bloomers, old chum, she's a bigger girl than that. No, it's been building up
for some time, hasn't it? She had a chat to me a year ago, initially. Anyway,
you'll be hearing from us about it. I could get one of my partners to
represent you but I think you owe it to yourself really to get some outside
help on this. I think Linzi will probably come in fairly heavily. After all,
it's nearly eight years. That's a long time in show business.
Charlie Yes.
Hugo She'll need a bit of financial help with the kids as well, of course.
Anyway. I thought I should give you a bit of advance warning. The press
are obviously going to perk up and show their customary concern, I should
imagine.
Charlie I should imagine.
Hugo Still, what is it they say in your business? The only bad publicity is no
publicity. Isn't that what you say?
Charlie Possibly. I've never heard anyone say it, but possibly.
Hugo Certainly true in my line. Tell you what, if you do need someone to
hold your jacket, you could do worse than sound out old Simeon, you

know. He's not the brightest bulb in the awning but he's as honest as the day. See you later, Charlie. Love to stay and chat but I'm due at the studio, unfortunately. I don't know why we agree to do these bloody programmes half the time, do you? Anyway, glad we sorted out that other business.

Charlie Yes.

Hugo waves his arm to someone in the garden. He gives a thumbs-up

Hugo Chin up now, old chum. Not like you to be down, is it?

From the garden, a small helicopter is heard to start up and tick over

(*Moving off*) Not you, Charlie. Always land on your feet, you do. Charmed life, eh? Cheerio!

Charlie (*as Hugo goes*) Hugo …

Hugo Yes?

Charlie You're not really gay, are you?

Hugo God, I hope not. I don't think that would go down too well with Imogen, would it?

Hugo goes off into the garden

Charlie sits watching him. From the garden, the helicopter continues to tick over

Linzi enters from the house. She doesn't immediately see Charlie as she is more interested in attracting the attention of the helicopter

Linzi (*waving as she enters, calling*) Hugo! Hugo! Hugo …

The sound of the helicopter taking off and moving away can be heard

(*Giving up*) Oh. (*She turns to go back and sees Charlie*) I thought you'd gone with Jason.

Charlie Oh, he's gone, has he?

Linzi I see that woman's been taking her clothes off again.

Charlie Right.

Linzi Torn her bra this time. I wasn't going to lend her one.

The helicopter has gone

I just wanted a word with Hugo.

Charlie About the divorce, was it?

Linzi He told you, did he?

Charlie Would have been nice to hear it from you, really.

Linzi Would it?

Charlie Well, it's not nice to hear from anybody, but …

Linzi I won't rip you off, Charlie, I promise. I could do, but I won't. You know I'd never do that to you. I wouldn't let Hugo do that, either. We've been through too much together for that, haven't we? I just need enough, you know, to get restarted. Make sure the kids are all right, you know.

Silence

Look at it positively. You'll be free as well.

Charlie Free to do what? Career's down the pan, isn't it? Everyone's pulling out. Now you're off …

Linzi I can't live like this any longer, Charlie. I can't live with myself like this. I can feel it, I'm turning into a right miserable old bag, I can feel it. I'm starting to hate myself, really. You wouldn't want to live with me much longer, not the way I am at the moment. No, I can't stand on the sidelines any more. I've got to be up there doing it. Being someone again. You understand that, don't you?

Charlie We can do that together. There's no need to split up, is there?

Linzi (*starting off towards the house*) Charlie! You're a celebrity, darling. I can't compete with that. (*As she goes*) I'm just a telly presenter. You're a star, Charlie, a star! Always will be!

Linzi goes off to the house

Charlie (*gloomily*) Twinkle! Twinkle!

He continues to sit there as ——

The Lights fade to Black-out

Curtain

Scene 2

The same. It is several months later, midwinter in fact: a cold, frosty day in January

When the Curtain *rises the garden is lit with a cold wintry light*

Charlie and Jason enter from the garden. They are well wrapped up, on a walk together

Jason ... it's funny seeing it all shut up like that, the house. It was always so busy, wasn't it? Bustling with people.

Charlie Yes, well, with only me, you know, and the housekeeper. No point, is there? I live in one room, practically, these days.

Jason But you say you think you've sold it?

Charlie At last. Had to drop a bit.

Jason I'm amazed. Celebrity's mansion. You'd think someone would snap it up.

Charlie Ex-celebrity.

Jason Matter of time, boy. I tell you, matter of time.

There is a slight pause

You going to miss it? Here?

Charlie Not really. Too many memories. Linzi. The kids. Funnily enough, I'll miss this place more than the house.

Jason Memories here, aren't there?

Charlie Nice ones mostly. Mostly.

Jason Ah.

There is a slight pause. Jason stares upward

Ever get to the top, did you?

Charlie What? Up there? No. It's all legend. No way up there. Short of flying.

Jason Nice to have climbed it once, wouldn't it? Shame.

Pause

Seen Linzi lately?

Charlie She's dropped in once or twice. Pick up some more of her things. She's slowly disappearing. Her and the kids. Pretty soon there won't be a trace of them left. Like they'd never been here.

Pause

You know, I sometimes wonder, Jason, when they vanish. When the last trace of them, Linzi and the kids, has gone, whether I'll vanish as well.

Jason How do you mean?

Charlie Just — disappear. Spontaneously. I mean, some people, they have a very strong presence, don't they? Know what I mean? They come in a room and you immediately know they're there. They register, you know. You see them at once. Whereas other people, people like me, we rely on other people to tell you we're there. Like — there's black holes — you know, like neutron stars — I was reading an article about this — and they're invisible. But the scientists, they know they're there, they deduce they're there, not because they can see them, but because of all the other visible stars round them behaving peculiarly. And that's how people knew I was there, you know. Because of everyone else around me behaving peculiarly. But once you take those people away, the visible stars, then all you've got left is an invisible black hole. Me. I'll still be here. But since no one will ever know, I might just as well not be, you see? You follow?

Jason considers this for a moment or two

Jason (*at last*) No, I don't know what you're talking about, Charlie.

There is a slight pause

Linzi's doing well, isn't she? You seen her? On *Skippitydoodah*?
Charlie No.
Jason Oh, you should try and catch her, Charlie. She's doing well. Like she'd never been away.
Charlie I'm glad.
Jason I'm glad I got her that. Course it helped a bit with her being Mrs Charlie Conrad. That helped.
Charlie The ex-Mrs Charlie Conrad.
Jason What with her being, you know, the innocent wronged party, so to speak. Not that she was wronged. Don't get me wrong.
Charlie No.
Jason Just that the perception was ... But I say to people, if she was wronged, she'd never have changed her name to Linzi Conrad-Ellison, would she?
Charlie Probably not. Whose idea was that, by the way?
Jason (*modestly*) Well, I think it was — mine, actually. But I can't take all the credit. It was a stroke of luck Melanie Messina dropping out like that.
Charlie Not for Melanie.
Jason No, six years. Poor girl. I wouldn't wish that on anyone. Gale must miss her.
Charlie She does.
Jason Really? How do you know? Why, have you seen her? Gale? I thought she'd dropped out of sight.
Charlie No, she's still working. Freelance.
Jason What, TV?
Charlie Newspapers.
Jason Oh.

Pause

Charlie Matter of fact, she's coming today.

Jason What?

Charlie She — asked me if she could do an interview.

Jason And what did you say?

Charlie I said she could.

Jason Oh, for crying ——

Charlie She needs the break, Jason ——

Jason — you owe that woman nothing, son ——

Charlie — she's having a rough time since Melanie went away and ——

Jason — less than nothing. She landed you in it. She deserved all she got. She spent her whole career pissing on people and now someone's shat on her in turn and serve her bloody right, she had it coming, mate. She's been and gone.

Charlie Yes, well, yesterday's people need to stick together, Jason. I'm hardly spoilt for choice. You haven't fixed me up with anything of late, have you? There's not that many journalists queuing up round the estate these days, are there? Not even for the where are they now page.

There is a slight pause

Jason What's she interviewing you about, then?

Charlie (*indicating the Tower*) About all this, what else?

Jason It's forgotten.

Charlie It's not forgotten.

Jason Forgotten!

Charlie If it's forgotten, why does everyone keep remembering it? She's going to give me the chance, just for once, to tell my version. Ever since that woman brought her book out …

Jason *Death of a Clown.*

Charlie Best-seller, isn't it? So I read. Every programme I switch on, she seems to be on it. Kid's programmes, gardening shows, celebrity sex-lines, topless chefs, I don't know … Marsha this. Marsha that.

Jason Five-minute wonder.

Charlie Maybe. Anyway, I'm doing an interview.

Jason With Gale Gilchrist?

Charlie I'm going to tell it exactly as it was.

Jason Good luck.

There is a slight pause

Look, what I wanted to talk to you about — why I came to see you, Charlie — listen, I'm thinking of jacking it in, actually. You know, stopping it all. Retiring. I've been thinking about it for some time. I'm getting a bit tired. I'm not as sharp as I was, you know.

Charlie Ah.

Jason I mean, I'll still be around for you — and for Linzi — if you both want me to — but with things, you know, like slowing down a bit for you ——

Charlie Like stopping altogether ——

Jason — temporarily. It seemed a good time for me to bow out.

Charlie I see.

Jason So.

Pause

Charlie I'll miss you.

Jason I'll still see you. I'm not going far.

Charlie Where you going?

Jason We were thinking of Jersey.

Charlie Jersey?

Jason Judy rather fancies Jersey. She doesn't like abroad, you see. It's too hot and the food's not so good.

Charlie What you going to do in Jersey all day?

Jason (*a little embarrassed*) Well. As a matter of fact, they've asked me if I'd write this book.

Charlie Oh, yes?

Jason Sort of memoirs, you know.

Charlie Memoirs?

Jason Reminiscences, you know. Nothing much.

Charlie About me?

Jason Well, you'd come into it. You're bound to come into it, Charlie. I mean you've been an important part of my life, haven't you? I could hardly leave you out, could I? But I'd cover other things. Not just you. Not *just* you. Early days as well, you know. Like when I worked at Butlins. Meeting Judy. Linzi. All that. Plenty of other stuff, as well. Mitzi. Our dog. Remember?

Charlie Yes, don't forget the dog.

Pause

Jason I'll tell it — like it was. Don't worry.

Pause

So, anyway, I ——

Gale appears from the direction of the house. A rather toned-down, less glamorous Gale from the one we first saw. We sense she's been through rather a lot since then. She carries a large hold-all

(*With some relief*) Oh! Look who's here!

Gale Hallo!

Jason Here she is. Gale!

Gale Jason! Hardly recognized you. I didn't know you'd be here.

Jason Just leaving, I'm literally just leaving, Gale, I just dropped in for a word with ——

Gale Hallo, Charlie! Lovely to see you.

Charlie Hallo, Gale.

They embrace

Gale God. The old place, eh?

Charlie Yes.

Gale The old place.

Charlie Yes. The same old place.

Pause

Jason Well, I must — if you'll both excuse me — I promised ...

Gale How's Judy?

Jason Oh, she's well. Thank you for asking, Gale. Yes, very well. And how's — everything?

Gale Fine,

Jason Good. Good. Glad to hear that. Yes. Well, I'll see you both, then. Love you and leave you. (*Heading towards the house*) As I say, Charlie, I won't be far away. I'll never be far away.

Charlie Cheers, Jason.

Jason goes off towards the house

Gale He's a nice man, isn't he? Really nice?

Charlie Yes, he's very nice.

Gale I heard he's retiring.

Charlie Oh, you heard that?

Gale You'll miss him, won't you?

Charlie I expect so.

Gale Listen, I won't keep you long. As I say, I'm doing this purely on spec. I normally wouldn't consider doing that, but I do think it's important that this story of yours gets written. And published. I've never felt so strongly about anything in my life, Charlie. I mean, you have been rubbished by this woman — this clown — this talentless nobody — Now she's *everywhere*, can you believe it?

Charlie I know.

Gale I despair, Charlie. What's happening to the world, eh? And you know why? How she got there, don't you? Only because of you, Charlie. She's used you, that's what she's done. Used — a real star like you — a genuine star — to launch her own pathetic little piss-pot career. But without you she'd never have existed, would she? No one would even want to know her. What is she? A cross-dressing clown who gets herself groped by a mega-star ——

Charlie (*wearily*) It wasn't like that ——

Gale — and then runs screaming all the way to the tabloids. Let's face it, she is nothing. She has no charisma, no talent, no personality, no star quality … no, don't get me started. Don't get me started on her. Anyway, the great thing about this, Charlie, is that, glory be, I am freelance again. That's how I started my life, Charlie, and that's how I'll finish. Never again. I can write what I like, say what I like, without some terrified producer, some paranoid editor telling me what I should or shouldn't say. God, after all those years — the freedom, Charlie, you can't imagine. It's like having to talk in a whisper for ten years and then suddenly finding, after all this time, I can shout again. (*Loudly*) Yes! Fantastic! *Yes!*

Charlie is becoming a trifle concerned. This is fairly manic, even by Gale's standards

Oh, yes, you fight them, of course you fight them, but in the end it's so tiring, you get so tired, Charlie, you've no idea. After three years doing the *Gale Gilchrist Show*, live, week after week — four series, Charlie, I was into the fourth series, did you know that? Four series, can you imagine that? Forty-five weeks every year, that's twenty-two and a half hours of live programmes for three and a half years. Live. That's seventy-eight and a half hours of live television …

Charlie (*overwhelmed a little by all this*) Wow! I didn't realize you ——

Gale And eventually I said to myself, that's it!" I said to myself, Gale, you either stop here and now or you have a serious breakdown, girl. And I stopped. I took a deep breath and I stopped. And people said to me, you're *mad*, you're *crazy*, Gale. Your viewing figure is off the scale, your ratings have never been higher … But I knew, Charlie, that if I didn't stop … then I … And I walked away, Charlie. Don't believe what you read. No one pushed me. I walked away, a free woman. And I've never looked back.

Charlie Good.

Silence

Gale Listen, I need to take some pictures, if that's OK. I brought my camera, I hope you don't mind. I'd normally, in normal circumstances, I'd bring a proper photographer only ... But I think the personal touch is so important, don't you? Yes.

There is a slight pause

Look, I'll show you. I hope you think this is a good idea ... I'm quite excited about it. (*She opens the bag and produces a clown's costume — trousers, jacket, wig, shoes — similar, but not identical, to those worn by Marsha earlier*) Look! Look! Here, you see. It's a clown's costume, I rented it from this shop. I had this idea, Charlie, of having you sitting here, where it — where it all happened — with the clown's costume sort of strewn round you — you know, like wreckage.

Charlie Wreckage?

Gale Yes, symbolic, you know.

Charlie Symbolic wreckage?

Gale Do you think it's all right?

Charlie (*uncertainly*) We can give it a go.

Gale I mean, it'll mainly be the interview but these days they always insist on a picture. People these days, they can't relate to anything that hasn't got pictures and words of two syllables ... most of them. It's soul-destroying, Charlie, it really is. What's happening to this country, do you know? (*She looks as if she might cry*)

Charlie Well, I don't know. Have things changed that much? I mean ——

Gale (*recovering slightly*) I'm just thinking, Charlie. Perhaps we should do the picture first? While the light's good. And then we can — we can — we can ... (*She tails off, then busies herself moving the furniture and props. She is fast falling apart at the seams*) Look, if we have the chair here — no, here, here's better. You sitting here and then we'll put all the bits around you. Or maybe against the pillar. What do you think? Against the pillar? (*Trying to move a pillar*) Do these move at all? No, of course, they wouldn't. I'll move the chair. It's easier to move the chair, isn't it? (*Turning her attention again to the clown's costume*) Now we need this, sort of strewn, you know. Sort of strewn ... like ... wreckage ... like ... (*She is now crying openly*)

Charlie looks at Gale with some concern

Charlie You want to sit down a minute?

Gale No, it's all right, it's all right.

Charlie You sure?

Gale No, I sometimes get ... (*She stands*)

Charlie watches her anxiously. Silence. When Gale speaks again it is in a smaller voice. Almost childlike

Gale I've just been … to … see her. That's all. That always makes me cry a bit. Sorry. She's there all on her own, you know. I go to see her and she's so frightened …

Charlie Melanie?

Gale She's only a kid, Charlie, a little kid. She shouldn't be there at all. It's such a terrible place, you've no idea. It's a horrible place. And she's so frightened. You've no idea. I just wanted to hold her. Hold her for a minute. Try and make her better. But they wouldn't even let me … touch her … you see …

Charlie steps forward and takes her in his arms. She clings to him for support. They stand there. Charlie, waiting for Gale to recover, looks rather awkward and helpless

Linzi enters. Seeing the tableau, she stops and waits. Linzi, despite yet another dramatic change of hair colour, looks a whole lot better, younger and livelier, almost girlish. Her new career has obviously revitalized her

Gale (*eventually recovering a little*) I'm sorry. (*She catches sight of Linzi and abruptly pulls away from Charlie*) Sorry. I just need to get one or two more things from my car.

With a somewhat hostile look at Linzi, Gale hurries away towards the house without looking back. She exits

Charlie When did you get here?

Linzi I just dropped by. Harry wanted something, I've been trying to find it. I thought it was in the barn there, but …

Charlie What's he want?

Linzi That little car of his, you know.

Charlie What, the petrol one?

Linzi Right.

Charlie It's in the garage. Back of the garage.

Linzi First place to look, of course.

Charlie The electric one I put in one of the spare rooms.

Linzi No, it's the petrol one. He wants the petrol one.

Pause

She all right, is she?

Charlie I don't think so. Melanie, you know. And all that.

Linzi Oh, yes. Sad. Lesson there for us all, isn't there?

Charlie What's that?

Linzi Never believe your own publicity. Believing you can walk on water still doesn't mean you can't drown. Even on dry land.

Charlie Ah.

Linzi Also, if you're going to take serious drugs then don't shack up with your dealer. What's she doing here, anyway?

Charlie An interview.

Linzi With you?

Charlie Yes.

Linzi Oh. Didn't realise she was still employable. What company's employing her, then?

Charlie It's not TV, it's newspapers.

Linzi Oh. Going to say. (*Indicating the clown's regalia*) What's all that?

Charlie For the picture.

Linzi Seriously?

Charlie Yes, seriously.

Linzi I hope you know what you're doing, Charlie.

Pause

Charlie You're looking good.

Linzi Thank you.

Charlie Changed your hair.

Linzi Well, it's for the programme, you know. My bid to look younger, you know.

Charlie You look about ten.

Linzi Oh, yes?

Charlie You look wonderful.

Linzi (*smiling*) Thank you.

Charlie smiles at her. A pause

Charlie Programme's going all right, I hear? *Skippitydoodah*?

Linzi Oh, yes. Pretty well. For a kids' programme, you know.

A slight pause

Oh. I think you ought to know, Charlie, I'm having her on the programme in a couple of weeks. In case you're watching. You know — Marsha Bates.

Charlie Are you?

Linzi I mean, I didn't want her on, not at all. But the producer, you know, insisted so … Sorry.

Charlie That's all right.

Linzi Just as a guest. Just the one-off. Mind you, I don't think our budget could afford her more than once anyway. She's the hottest thing since … since the last hottest thing.

Charlie (*murmuring*) Me. Probably.

Pause

Linzi (*with a slight smile*) See you around, then.

Charlie See you around.

Linzi (*as she goes*) Glad they're asking for interviews again, anyway, Charlie, that's a good sign, isn't it?

Charlie Sure.

Linzi I said you wouldn't be out for long, didn't I? Bye, bye, love!

Linzi goes off towards the house

Charlie watches her rather sadly. He picks up part of the clown's outfit and studies it. He smiles and shakes his head

Laura and Katie, the two young girls, come on quietly wearing their winter coats, gloves, boots and hats. They watch Charlie solemnly

Charlie doesn't immediately notice the girls

Charlie (*seeing them at last*) Hey, what are you two doing here? You shouldn't be here, surely? Your mum doesn't allow you in here, does she? I'm sure she doesn't. How'd you get in, then? Climb through the fence, I bet? I bet you did. Didn't you?

The girls continue to stare impassively at him

Here! Here! Tell you what. Want so see something funny, do you? Want to have a laugh? Here, wait, I'll give you a laugh. Just a tick. Wait there, wait a second. (*He puts on elements of the clown's costume. Perhaps not all of it, but certainly the wig and funny trousers*)

The girls continue to stare, unmoved

Here watch this, then! Watch this! Watch the funny man! (*He goes through an improvised clown routine. He does his best but, since it's Charlie, it really isn't very funny. He gets quite carried away. Busily improvising his act*) Hey! Hup! Woooh! Hey! Aaah! (*etc.*)

The girls remain unsmiling. Charlie moves closer to Laura and Katie in an effort to involve them. Katie screams. Laura follows suit

The girls rush off, still screaming in (apparent) terror

Charlie (*as they both flee from him*) Hey! It's OK! Don't be ... I'm not going to ... I wouldn't ... Hey! (*He slowly removes the clown's gear and discards it. Sadly*) Oh, well. (*He wanders to the mouth of the archway where the stairs lead upwards. To himself*) Here goes. One more time ...

He hesitates, then goes out

The stage is empty and still for a second. Then, all at once, it starts to lighten and there is the bright sound of winter birdsong. The Tower is now lit with brilliant early-afternoon January sunlight

Charlie steps out from the other archway and finds himself at the top of the tower. He stands there incredulously, staring about him, marvelling at the view and his own achievement.

(*At last, softly*) Oh, my God! (*With a growing joy*) I made it! I did it! I did it!

As he stands there smiling ——

The Lights fade to Black-out

Curtain

FURNITURE AND PROPERTY LIST

ACT I

On stage: Three or four good-quality garden chairs
Low table

Off stage: Prop hamper (**Marsha**)
Large suitcase (**Marsha**)

Personal: **Charlie**: mobile phone, pen
Jason: mobile phone, small recording device
Gale: handbag containing small recording device
Marsha: prop flower

ACT II

Off stage: Large hold-all containing clown's costume (**Gale**)

Personal: **Jason**: notebook, pen

LIGHTING PLOT

Practical fittings required: nil
One exterior. The same throughout

ACT I

To open: General exterior lighting; bright summer sunshine

Cue 1	**Charlie**: "Oh, no …" Pause *Fade to black-out*	(Page 32)

ACT II, Scene 1

To open: General exterior lighting; bright summer sunshine

Cue 2	**Charlie**: "Twinkle! Twinkle!" *Fade to black-out*	(Page 49)

ACT II, Scene 1

To open: General exterior lighting; cold, wintry light

Cue 3	**Charlie** exits. Pause *Brighten lights to brilliant early-afternoon January sunlight*	(Page 60)
Cue 4	**Charlie**: "I did it! I did it!" Pause *Fade to black-out*	(Page 60)

EFFECTS PLOT

ACT I

Cue 1 **Jason**: "Suits you. That colour." Pause (Page 10)
    Mobile phone ring

Cue 2 **Jason**: "… ask the public." Pause (Page 22)
    Distant children's cheer

Cue 3 **Gale**: "Isn't it? On the winners?" Silence (Page 24)
    Distant children's cheer

Cue 4 **Gale**: " … the same place you started." (Page 24)
    Distant children's cheer

Cue 5 **Charlie**: "I feel real enough, Gale." (Page 24)
    Mobile phone ring

Cue 6 **Jason** and **Gale** exit. Pause (Page 27)
    Loud cheering and applause

ACT II

Cue 7 **Hugo**: " … to be down, is it?" (Page 48)
    Sound of small helicopter starting up and ticking over
     (continuous until next cue)

Cue 8 **Linzi**: "Hugo! Hugo! Hugo!" (Page 48)
    Helicopter takes off and moves away

Cue 9 **Linzi**: "I wasn't going to lend her one." (Page 48)
    Helicopter sound fades to silence

Cue 10 Lights brighten (Page 60)
    Bright sound of winter birdsong